By
Design
or
Accident

By
Design
or
Accident

Reflections
on
Asian Security

Daljit Singh

LSEAS

Institute of Southeast Asian Studies
Singapore

First published in Singapore in 2010 by ISEAS Publishing
Institute of Southeast Asian Studies
30 Heng Mui Keng Terrace
Pasir Panjang
Singapore 119614

E-mail: publish@iseas.edu.sg
Website: <http://bookshop.iseas.edu.sg>

The responsibility for facts and opinions in this publication rests exclusively with the author and his interpretations do not necessarily reflect the views or the policy of the publisher or its supporters.

ISEAS Library Cataloguing-in-Publication Data

Daljit Singh.
   By design or accident : reflections on Asian security.
   1. National security—Asia.
   2. Political stability—Asia.
   3. Asia—Strategic aspects.
   I. Title.
UA830 D14   2010

ISBN 978-981-4279-71-0 (hard cover)
ISBN 978-981-4279-72-7 (E-Book PDF)

Typeset by Superskill Graphics Pte Ltd
Printed in Singapore by Fabulous Printers Pte Ltd

Contents

Foreword

It gives me great pleasure to write the Foreword to this collection of thoughtful essays written by my good friend and high school classmate, Daljit Singh.

Daljit and I were classmates at Raffles Institution, from 1952 to 1957. He was one of the top students of the school. After completing his university education, he joined the civil service and served in several senior positions. Daljit has always had a scholarly inclination and it was therefore natural for him to transit from the civil service to the Institute of Southeast Asian Studies. At the Institute he has been the editor of *Southeast Asian Affairs*, the prestigious annual review of the region, and of other scholarly publications; the convener of various conferences and seminars; and a security analyst and commentator on trends and developments in the relations between States in Southeast Asia, Asia and the world.

This book contains thirty-seven essays written by Daljit Singh between 1991 and 2009. They were originally published either in Singapore or in the *International Herald Tribune*. Although I had read the essays when they were first published, I have enjoyed reading them again, partly because of their enduring merit and partly because the author has wisely organised them into four parts. In this way, one is better able to appreciate the coherence and continuity of the author's worldview and his thought process in following the evolution of a situation, for example, the war in Iraq, over a number of years.

Part I of the book contains nine essays on Southeast Asia and regional security after the Cold War. The essay on Myanmar, although written in 1994, is still relevant today: "Solutions to Myanmar's problems will have to be found by the Myanmar people themselves. Outsiders can only encourage or discourage certain trends …. The isolation of the regime and the suspension of aid have not succeeded in getting it to change its mind, let alone remove it from power …. Some form of political evolution is required for stability and progress. If the new political system envisaged by SLORC (SPDC) can provide this evolution, even with limited democracy and openness, it would constitute movement in the right direction …"

The essay which I found most fascinating is the one on the democratic peace theory and Asia, written in 1998. It is often claimed by the proponents of democracy that one of its virtues is that democracies do not go to war with each other. In this essay, Daljit Singh asked whether the theory could apply to Asia. In his view, war between a "democratic" India and a "democratic" Pakistan is not unthinkable. The author argued that both India and Pakistan were weak democracies, with deficiences in the rule of law and extensive poverty and illiteracy. He seemed to imply that the democratic peace theory only applies to mature democracies.

Part II of the book contains eleven essays on terrorism and the war in Iraq. The most important essay is the 2008 essay on how Southeast Asia has succeeded in keeping terrorism at bay.

Part III of the book, "The Big Boys of Asian Geopolitics", is, for me, the most important section of the book. In these essays, the author discusses the evolving geopolitical and geoeconomic order of the Asia-Pacific region. I agree with the author that, for the foreseeable future, the United States will remain the dominant power of the region. However, the United States will have to share the stage with the two rising Asian giants, China and India, as well as with a "new" Japan in search of a new role and identity and a resurgent Russia. The author is right to call this the "major drama" of the 21st century. The essay, "ASEAN as a Geopolitical Player", is a useful reminder to all the ASEAN-sceptics of the vital role which ASEAN plays in this new Asian drama as the region's convener, facilitator and catalyst.

I commend this book and wish it success.

Tommy Koh
Chairman
Institute of Policy Studies
Singapore
December 2009

Introduction

Asia is rising and will wield greater economic and strategic weight in world affairs. However, Asia also faces numerous challenges like poverty, domestic instability, deficiencies in governance and the rule of law, interstate disputes and rivalries, and military build-ups, to name just a few. The celebration of Asia's rise would be premature if it is not accompanied by lasting peace and cooperation between states and justice and prosperity at home. The achievement of this happy state of affairs will require wise and pragmatic leadership, especially among the major powers.

This book is a compilation of my opinion pieces over the years which first appeared in the Singapore *Straits Times*, *Business Times*, *International Herald Tribune*, and *ISEAS Trends*. By their very nature as occasional opinion pieces, they do not pretend to provide a comprehensive picture of the events and issues they deal with. For a long time it had not occurred to me to compile them into a book. It was Professor Tommy Koh who persuaded me to do so. In an age already surfeit with books of varying quality, I would like to believe that this thin volume will provide some feel and flavour of the events and times it depicts.

The title *By Design or Accident* suggests that history is shaped both by human design and by fortuitous circumstances. The role of leadership, both state and non-state, is undeniably important. Yet unintended consequences or completely unanticipated developments can make a mockery of the most carefully worked out plans of human genius, whether benign or malign.

The book is divided into a number of parts by theme, with the opinion pieces under each theme arranged chronologically. Inevitably there are pieces which do not fit comfortably into these neat categories. Also, some overlap across sections has been unavoidable.

Part I contains pieces written mostly between the end of the Cold War and the 9/11 attacks on the United States, although it also includes two on ASEAN which were written later. The period was marked by regional rapprochement, the establishment of the ASEAN Regional Forum, concerns about the future of the American military presence in Asia, and anxieties about how a rising China could be accommodated into the regional and international systems. ASEAN's international standing fluctuated from a peak attained around 1995 to a low in the wake of Asian crisis. It was also a period when American policy to the region saw a stronger push for democratization.

Part II of the book covers two major conflicts of the first decade of the new century, the struggle against Al Qaeda-linked terrorism and the Iraq war. Iraq and terrorism were two separate phenomena when Saddam Hussain was in power but became partially fused into one as a result of the American invasion. During this period, the security policies of the Administration of President George W. Bush were widely seen as unilateralist and driven by right-wing ideologues. As can be seen in the pieces on the Iraq war, my own thinking on the war evolved quickly from support to deep misgivings as I realized how badly the US Administration had misjudged what it would take to bring change for the better in Iraq. This section also includes two articles on Southeast Asia's efforts to deal with terrorism.

Part III contains writings on the big players in Asian geopolitics, namely, America, China, Japan, and India. The rise of new Asian powers and their interactions with each other and with the "established" powers will be a major drama of the 21ˢᵗ century which will have a crucial bearing on the prospects for Asia. The reader may notice that concern about the balance of power in Asia has been a recurrent underlying theme in my opinion pieces, even when addressing issues like the Iraq war, the war on terrorism, and Sino-Vietnamese relations. Also in Part III is a piece on the Australia-Indonesia security treaty. It does not fit neatly into any of the parts, but is placed here for its possible broader geopolitical significance in relation to the major powers.

Finally, there is a Part IV of just two articles which did not fit into any of the first three parts. These recall two important conflicts of the past, the Malayan Emergency and the Vietnam War, and seek to show their historical importance.

I am indebted first and foremost to Professor Tommy Koh for encouraging me to publish this book and for graciously offering to write the Foreword. I thank Ambassador Kesavapany, Director of ISEAS, for his support and for encouraging ISEAS researchers to reach out to a wider audience by contributing opinion pieces in the press. I also thank ISEAS Publications Unit, in particular its head, Mrs Triena Ong, for managing the production aspects of this book.

Daljit Singh
Institute of Southeast Asian Studies
December 2009

PART I

Southeast Asia and Regional Security after the Cold War

1
Sino-Vietnamese Reconciliation: Cause for Celebration?

The chain reactions produced by the ending of the Cold War and the vast changes in the Soviet Union over the last few years are still working themselves through Asia. In Southeast Asia they are producing another turn of the geopolitical kaleidoscope.

The changes in Soviet policy, including the drastic reduction of aid to Vietnam, are forcing Hanoi to come to terms with China, its giant neighbour to the north with which, until recently, relations had been one of bitter enmity. And with Vietnam thus in dire straits and the Soviet threat to China much diminished, Beijing, for its part, sees this as an opportune time to strike a deal with Hanoi on important issues.

Events in Eastern Europe and the Soviet Union, too, are driving Vietnam and China closer. The elderly leaders of both states have watched the turmoil there with horror and seem determined to prevent at all costs its occurrence in their own countries. Both have agreed that while economic reform must continue, political pluralism cannot be permitted. Communist party rule must be preserved.

What will be the implications for Southeast Asia of a thaw in Sino-Vietnamese relations?

Firstly, there is likely to be a settlement of the Cambodian conflict where China and Vietnam have been the principal backers of the resistance and the Phnom Penh government, respectively. Both countries seem to have decided for their own reasons that it is time to settle the matter, though difficult negotiations may still lie ahead.

A final settlement will obviously have to be a compromise which is acceptable to both the Chinese and the Vietnamese. Beijing is committed to ensuring that the Khmer Rouge is not excluded but seems prepared to put pressure on it to go along with compromises worked out between the Sihanouk faction and Hun Sen. In the end, the Khmer Rouge may be increasingly marginalised.

Secondly, the chances of a conflict in the Spratlys will probably diminish because Vietnam and China were the two claimants most likely to have started one. The Spratlys issue will still pose dangers and it will be difficult to resolve in a manner acceptable to all parties because of the number of conflicting sovereignty claims, but the chances of it being contained will now improve.

Thirdly, Vietnam will have to give up its ambition to control Indochina. It is already clear that it cannot sustain control of Laos and Cambodia in the face of China's opposition without external big power backing, which until now was from the Soviet Union. We can, therefore, expect the emergence of three relatively independent Indochinese states.

Fourthly, if all the above come to pass, China's standing and influence in the countries of Indochina, and by extension in Southeast Asia, will be enhanced. Hanoi will be paying more heed to China's vital interests and sensitivities, and Beijing will be enjoying significantly more political influence in Laos and Cambodia than it does today.

In spite of Vietnam and China's newfound common interests, Hanoi will remain wary of too close an embrace of Beijing, and will seek room for manoeuvre through ties with other countries. Moreover, China cannot provide the economic aid and investments that Vietnam needs for its economic reform programme to succeed. They will have to come from other sources once the US embargo is lifted.

So, increased Chinese influence in Indochina may have no significant impact at this stage on the balance of power in the Southeast Asian region as a whole, where, among the external powers, China's presence and influence will be offset by those of the US and Japan. Nevertheless, any enhancement of China's naval and air capabilities in the coming years will be closely watched by countries in the region in view of China's proximity, and its extensive claims in the South China Sea.

On the whole the improvement in Sino-Vietnamese relations and the end of the Cambodian conflict will constitute positive developments for the Southeast Asian region. For the first time in nearly half a century there will be peace in Indochina, followed by normalisation of political and economic relations between the three countries and the rest of the international community, including the Asean states. If all goes well, Indochina will experience the rapid economic growth and progress which have eluded it so far.

Note

This article first appeared in *ISEAS Trends*, July 1991, under the title "Sino-Vietnamese Embrace: Cause for Celebration?".

2
Asia-Pacific Security Comes under ASEAN's Scrutiny

For much of its 25-year existence, ASEAN was extremely reluctant to openly identify itself with security concerns because it did not want to be seen as taking sides in the Cold War.

This has changed with the end of the Cold War. ASEAN has now shown active interest in not just Southeast Asian but also broader Asia-Pacific security issues. The Singapore Declaration issued last year at the Fourth ASEAN Summit states that "ASEAN should intensify its external dialogues in political and security matters by using the ASEAN Post-Ministerial Conferences (PMC)."

Last month, senior ASEAN officials met their counterparts from the seven dialogue partners — the US, Japan, the European Community, South Korea, Canada, Australia and New Zealand — in a conference devoted exclusively to security matters. These discussions can be expected to continue during the ASEAN PMC next month. Indeed the PMC seems to be emerging as an important Asia-Pacific forum for security discussions.

Two inter-related questions arise. Why the need for an Asia-Pacific forum for discussions on security? What can it realistically achieve?

The simple answer to the first question is that there has so far been no forum where the countries of East Asia, the US, Canada, Australia and New Zealand can sit together to discuss security concerns. For reasons of history and heterogeneity, there has been no equivalent of either a collective defence alliance like the North Atlantic Treaty Organization (Nato) or a forum like the Conference on Security and Cooperation in Europe (CSCE).

Western Pacific security has rather been based on an American military presence and America's *bilateral* defence treaties and arrangements with various countries which were concluded in the earlier years of the Cold War to protect these countries from aggression by the Communist powers.

Many feel that this structure cannot by itself deal satisfactorily with all the problems of post-Cold War East Asia where, except on the Korean peninsula, there are now no clearly defined adversarial relationships. Although the Asia Pacific region is today more peaceful that at any other time since the end of the Second World War, there is disquiet that these good times will not last through the next decade if the strategic changes already in motion take an undesirable turn and produce new enmities and tensions.

On the big canvas, two matters are of particular concern in this respect. One is the reduction of US power. If the US draws down its military forces too drastically or loses its will to be the key player in the Western Pacific before a new balance can emerge peacefully, it is not difficult to foresee new China-Japan, Korea-Japan and India-China tensions and new pressures on Southeast Asia by rival powers.

The other is the rise of China. China is already showing signs of wanting to acquire a capability to project its power beyond its shores. How will this emergent new superpower relate to its neighbours in Asia?

The main purpose of a multilateral Asia-Pacific security forum would be to cushion the effects of potentially destabilizing changes that are now taking place. The hope is that, over a period of time, habits of consultation and co-operation will form and suspicions and tensions will be reduced. After all, ASEAN was able to mute differences and vastly improve relations among member countries through many informal contacts and quiet discussions.

Can ASEAN's experience be replicated for the entire Asia-Pacific region? The skeptics would say no, pointing to the differences in size, history and cultures, not to mention that ASEAN was galvanized to co-cooperate by the perception of a common enemy whereas an all-inclusive Asia-Pacific organisation would lack this singular "advantage".

The best argument for persisting on the course of multilateral Asia-Pacific security discussions is that there is no other alternative. We are all condemned to try to make it work, so high seem the stakes.

The fact that the Clinton Administration, unlike its predecessor, is supportive of multilateral security discussions should facilitate ASEAN's task. However, the present discussions are preliminary and exploratory. China and Russia are not ASEAN's dialogue partners and hence are not members of the PMC. A way will have to be found to bring them into a comprehensive Asia-Pacific forum.

But one thing is clear: Asia-Pacific multi-lateral security discussions can complement the existing security structure based on the US alliance system and the US military presence, but they cannot be a substitute for it. They will not go far if the existing structure were to collapse.

To expect the big and powerful to refrain from pushing and shoving to assert their "legitimate" interests when countervailing power is absent would be to expect too much a change in human nature or the behaviour of nation-states, rhetoric notwithstanding. It would be nice to believe that "balance of power" is an old-fashioned concept and security anxieties can be alleviated by purely paper agreements and confidence-building measures, but unfortunately this is not yet the case, and probably will not be until there is an effective international machinery to enforce agreements.

Note

This article first appeared in *ISEAS Trends*, June 1993.

3
East Asian Security Means Dialogue and US Will

Rapid growth is transforming the economic landscape of East Asia. Together with changes set in motion by the end of the Cold War, it will transform the strategic landscape as well, creating a need for new structures to maintain stability and defuse tensions.

The security problems today in East Asia pale compared with those faced by the region in the past. The area is more or less at peace for the first time since the end of World War II. But dangers lurk behind the great promise of East Asia and need wise management. The dangers are not imminent. They lie just over the horizon.

They arise from the shifting balance between the four major powers — the United States, Japan, China and Russia — whose interests intersect in East Asia. Will this equilibrium alter gradually over the next decades, or will there be precipitate changes?

Historical suspicions and rivalries between Asian nations were held in abeyance by the contest between the two super powers during the Cold War. They can quickly come to the fore again if there are sudden lurches in the regional power balance. The future of the US security presence and commitments will be the key.

If America is seen to be reducing its military forces too fast or losing its will to be a major player, it is likely that there will be new arms races and tensions between the main Asian powers, and new pressures on the smaller countries in the region.

China aspires to a large role in Asia as it rapidly gains economic power and upgrades its armed forces. The Japanese government watches this with unease that can turn into alarm and lead to rearmament if it loses confidence in the will or ability of the United States to protect Japan.

The joker in the pack, a North Korean nuclear bomb, can also push Japan toward an independent defense policy that would alarm other Asians. A sudden shift in the power balance would also increase the risk of conflict at potential flash points. What can be done to reduce the risks? First, there is a clear need for more multilateral political and security discussions to build trust and cooperation. Second, the main potential cause of destabilizing change, a US military withdrawal that is too fast, must be avoided.

New arrangements and institutions are needed, such as the security forum approved by the foreign ministers of seventeen Asia-Pacific nations at an informal dinner discussion in Singapore this past Sunday. The forum has been set up to nurture habits of consultation and cooperation among states in the region, including the United States, Canada, Australia and New Zealand.

Apart from ASEAN, there has been a lack of multilateral forums in the Asia-Pacific area for political and security discussions. Because of the region's history, size and diversity, there has been no equivalent of institutions in Europe like NATO, the Western European Union or the Conference on Security and Cooperation in Europe. Western

Pacific security has been based on an American military presence and a network of bilateral defense treaties and security cooperation arrangements with the United States.

Many in the region feel that this structure can no longer by itself deal satisfactorily with the problems of post-Cold War East Asia, where, except on the Korean Peninsula, there are now no clearly defined adversarial relationships. The new dialogue arrangement approved in Singapore on Sunday, which is to be called the ASEAN Regional Forum, could provide a mechanism not just for discussing problems but also for managing potential and actual crises. It can help to accommodate the rising power of China and Japan while integrating Russia and eventually a reunited Korea in the Asia-Pacific security order.

But new arrangements for cooperation and confidence-building can be successfully put in place only if America remains engaged militarily and economically. They can complement the existing security structure based on the US alliance systems, but they cannot be a substitute.

It would be nice to regard balance of power as an old-fashioned concept and expect security anxieties to be alleviated by verbal pledges and paper agreements. Unfortunately, this is not the case, and probably will not be until there is effective international machinery to enforce agreements.

US trade with Asia is now 40 per cent greater than US trade with Western Europe. The high-growth countries of Asia provide the best prospects for growth of American exports and jobs, and hence revival of the American economy. Yet there is still insufficient importance accorded to Asia in the United States.

Americans should not despair if many parts of East Asia do not fit into the American model of democracy and human rights. There is a need for perspective, historical and cultural. Economics and information will transform Asian societies in the direction favoured by the United States, although the change will sometimes follow a zigzag path.

The end product may be an amalgam of East and West, politically more open, tolerant and pluralistic but with an Asian style and flavor. The talk of a clash of civilizations between East Asia and the West is simplistic and betrays despair.

In Tokyo recently for the summit of the Group of Seven industrial powers, President Bill Clinton pledged to honor US security commitments to allies and friends in Asia. However, his new administration needs to forge a more coherent foreign policy, for there have been voices within the US government which suggest a decline in the will to exercise international leadership.

Also, as the US defense budget is cut, a new vocabulary has entered the public debate. Instead of playing a dominant role in East Asia, as in the past, America, some say, will be a "balancer"; it will side with one country or another to maintain a balance between rival powers.

Thus, despite the assurances of Clinton administration officials, some doubts still persist about the will of the United States to retain strong and credible military power in East Asia and the Western Pacific beyond this decade.

Note

This article first appeared in *International Herald Tribune*, 27 July 1993.

4
Where is Myanmar Headed?

In 1988, Myanmar abandoned the socialist path which, with its nationalisation and Burmanisation of the economy, had brought the country close to economic ruin. Since then, private enterprise has been encouraged, a liberal investment code established and there has been increase of trade, tourism and foreign investments. The process of economic reform seems irreversible.

However, economic performance has been below expectations for a country which claims to have abandoned socialism in favour of market economics more than five years ago, so much so that some analysts doubt that Myanmar has really come out of its economic stagnation. Vietnam, which embarked on its *doi moi* (reform) programme only a couple of years earlier, has done much better. For instance, foreign investments committed to Myanmar in financial year 1992–93 amounted to US$900 million (provisional figure) while over US$4 billion were committed to Vietnam in 1993.

Most of the investments to Myanmar are in extractive sectors like mining, forestry and fisheries, or in tourism-related projects like hotels. Foreign investors are reluctant to put their money into substantial fixed capital with long-term returns.

Vietnam's GDP has grown by an annual average rate of 4.4 per cent since 1986, compared with Myanmar's 0.5 per cent over the same period, and 4.8 per cent since 1988 compared with Myanmar's 1.5 per cent.

The explanation for this state of Myanmar's economic affairs lies not in the economics but in the politics of the country. Myanmar has not yet found a way out of the impasse it got itself into in 1988 when civilian opposition confronted the military regime resulting in violence, many deaths and the suspension of economic aid by the leading western powers and Japan.

The general elections in 1990 were supposed to resolve this impasse and produce a civilian government. But they did not because the pro-military political party, the National Unity Party, won only ten of the seats in the proposed 491-seat legislature while Aung San Suu Kyi's opposition National League for Democracy (NLD), espousing liberal democracy, won 392. It is not clear whether the military rulers had miscalculated or were forced by circumstances in 1988 to promise elections. Perhaps both. However, because of their fear that they would be held to account for the civilian deaths of 1988 and their apparent belief that NLD-type of democracy and federalism would bring ruin to the country, they were not prepared to surrender power to the NLD.

The State Law and Order Restoration Council (SLORC), the name by which the military rulers have called themselves since 1988, is supposed to be only a caretaker emergency government which assumed power after the political violence in 1988 with the stated aims of restoring law and order and holding multi-party elections. Since the fundamental political impasse has not been resolved and the events of

1988 and 1990 are still fresh in the minds of many people, investors see political risks in putting their money into long gestation projects. The economic sanctions applied by the western countries are also a serious disincentive to investors. The suspension of bilateral and multilateral aid has been a particularly serious blow to the Myanmar economy for the country has meager means of its own to upgrade its poor infrastructure.

The SLORC has thus been in a Catch-22 situation. It needs rapid economic growth to acquire political legitimacy. Yet political stability based on regime legitimacy seems to be a necessary precondition for the flow of significant aid and investments in manufacturing and agro-businesses.

SLORC has a plan to extricate itself from this impasse. A new constitution is being prepared which, it is said, will pave the way for an Indonesia-type system which allows for elections to a parliament while ensuring the dominance of the military in key policy-making and administrative institutions. The regime expects the implementation of such a political system, by providing at least formal regime legitimisation and some progress in democratisation, to strengthen the case for resumption of bilateral and multilateral aid by the major industrial powers and lending bodies. It hopes that at least Japan would resume ODA and that Japanese aid, together with better domestic stability and increased economic linkages with fast growing East and Southeast Asia, will then enable the Myanmar economy to take off which, in turn, will provide performance legitimacy to the government.

SLORC has no intention of allowing Aung San Suu Kyi to stand for any political office under the new system.

The new constitution will have clauses about domicile and marriage which will effectively bar her from doing so. She, of course, personifies the basic political Catch-22. Her release from detention and free circulation in Myanmar at this stage is seen as a serious threat to SLORC for she still commands popular support, though it may not be so visible on the surface.

SLORC fears that her presence will spark popular demonstrations. On the other hand continued detention undermines the legitimacy SLORC is trying so hard to achieve. And she refuses to be helpful by leaving the country. However, when the military feels more confident, perhaps some time after the establishment of the new political order, they may release her under certain conditions.

What are the chances of success for SLORC's strategy? There are several pitfalls on the road ahead.

The new constitution is being drafted under SLORC direction and guidance by carefully screened representatives of political parties and functional groups. It will have to pass some form of test of popular endorsement. It is not clear yet if SLORC will opt for a direct referendum, which may be risky. Even after the new constitution has been successfully implemented, with elections and a new government, the problem of legitimacy for the new government will not be entirely resolved. It will acquire *de jure* legitimacy but not yet one in the hearts and minds of the people.

It is unlikely that the US and the European Union will resume aid if SLORC, in setting up the new political order, shows no regard at all for the results of the 1990 election and allows no political role for Aung San Suu Kyi. Japan would be tempted to resume aid but it is not clear if it will be prepared to offend the Americans by succumbing to that temptation.

Will the Myanmar economy turn around under the new political order, assuming there is Japanese assistance, and with stronger economic links with East and Southeast Asia, as SLORC clearly hopes? The prospects seem fairly good, but only if the Myanmar military learns some other lessons from the Indonesian experience. The most important perhaps is the willingness to use economic experts and able administrators, to heed their advice and to give them enough leeway in their areas of expertise and management. To do this will require a basic change in the attitudes of the Myanmar military, given its past history of mistrust of those outside a small inner circle, its extreme unwillingness to share power and decision-making, and its fears about losing control.

There will also be other challenges. The economy will need more market-oriented reforms which will bring, at least in the short run, more inflation, unemployment and inequalities. Will the military have the courage to carry out these reforms? Will it have the communication and political management skills to deal with the resultant increase in public discontent? In spite of an elaborate security and information network, its knowledge of public attitudes, aspirations and likely reactions has at times been suspect. It cannot afford to make major errors of judgment as it has done before, for instance in carrying out the demonetisation exercise of 1987 which contributed to the build up of public anger that exploded into violence in 1988.

Solutions to Myanmar's problems will have to be found by the Myanmar people themselves. Outsiders can only encourage or discourage certain trends.

The isolation of the regime and the suspension of aid have not succeeded in getting it to change its mind, let alone removing it from power. This situation is not expected to change in the foreseeable future. The regime appears to be in a stronger position today than when economic sanctions were imposed in 1988. This resilience can be attributed to a number of factors, among them support from China, foreign exchange earnings acquired from sale of natural resources, the emasculation of organized Burman opposition and the deals cut with the ethnic insurgent groups to settle, for the time being, most of the insurgencies.

Asean's stance is that since efforts to isolate SLORC will not succeed in bending or breaking it, they will only prolong the economic travail of the Myanmar people. Some form of political evolution is required for stability and economic progress. If the new political system envisaged by SLORC can provide this evolution, even with limited democracy and openness, it would constitute movement in the right direction, especially since there is no other practical alternative.

Note

This article first appeared in *ISEAS Trends*, April 1994.

5
What Indonesian Stability Means to the ASEAN Region

Indonesian stability has been such an accepted phenomenon in the past thirty years that it has come to be taken for granted. It is, however, crucial to the region and to ASEAN.

After the abortive pro-communist coup of 30 September 1965, the new political forces headed by General Suharto moved quickly to seek regional reconciliation. Confrontation against Malaysia and Singapore was formally ended in 1966 and ASEAN was established in 1967. The birth of the regional grouping was above all an expression and a symbol of this reconciliation between regional neighbours. ASEAN has, of course, grown enormously in strength and influence since then.

A cursory look at the map would show the place Indonesia occupies in Southeast Asia, over nearly 50 degrees of longitude from west to east, by far the largest member of ASEAN both in land area and in population. But the size does not necessarily translate into commensurate influence in a regional organisation. On the contrary, size can arouse fears of domination among the smaller members, impeding rather than advancing regional cooperation.

How was it possible for ASEAN to build the level of intra-mural confidence that it now enjoys when one of its members was not only dominant in terms of size but had recently mounted a Confrontation policy against two of its neighbours?

The most important reason was that Indonesia, conscious of the burden of size and history, chose a low-key approach in its dealings with its ASEAN partners. It was able to show to them through word and practice that it had no wish to be a hegemon, that it valued consultations and consensus.

This was not a matter of tactical expediency. Indonesia was able to demonstrate to its ASEAN partners that it was willing to put on hold, for a long time to come, its regional ambitions for the sake of regional harmony and its own economic development. This self-denial was based on calculations of enlightened self-interest: influence commensurate with size would come naturally with economic success, within the frame-work of international rules and norms, and through acceptance of Indonesia's role by regional neighbours.

In ASEAN, no country claims to be a leader and that may be the secret of its success. But Indonesia has been a key player, the first among equals. Its voice has always carried weight, especially on issues of regional security and the development of regionalism.

Indonesia inspired confidence not just by its conduct in ASEAN and its bilateral relations towards neighbours. It did so also by the way it conducted its own national affairs from 1966. In New Order Indonesia, economics rather that politics was in command. Western trained economists were given the task of rescuing and then expanding the economy. They pursued rational economic policies which were subject to the usual constraints imposed by foreign governments and international bankers who provided the capital for rehabilitation and development. The result has been perhaps the most impressive economic success story in Asia.

Indonesia's military modernization over the years has been very restrained and modest. There have been no discernible impulses to match size with the most modern military forces. The bulk of the Indonesian armed forces still remain geared to internal security. This served to reinforce the perception of a country pursuing external policies of moderation and peace.

All this has been in sharp contrast to the early 1960s under the previous order when the emphasis was on political rhetoric and mobilization and military build-ups while the economy was run to the ground.

To achieve its economic development goals, the New Order had to curb the political excesses of the past and provide the necessary political stability for investors to put their money into the country. The formula by which politics was reordered for the sake of stability appears to have served Indonesia well for thirty years, transforming the economic and social landscape. In recent years, it has aroused criticism among Indonesians, with many arguing that the changed circumstances require a more flexible, open and responsive political system.

Thus, how Indonesia manages the transition to the post-Suharto period, even if, as expected, the President seeks and obtains another term in office in 1998, is of great importance to ASEAN, and in particular to Indonesia's immediate neighbors, Malaysia, Singapore and the Philippines.

Most observers of the Indonesian scene do not think that domestic events will affect the fundamentals of Indonesian policies in relation to ASEAN and Southeast Asia for they are accepted by the majority of the civilian and military elites in Jakarta.

Still, domestic developments will be watched closely by ASEAN neighbours, as well as by outside powers. As Indonesia itself has taught others, domestic instability drains national resilience and also weakens regional resilience. This would be especially so if the instability were to take place in a pivotal ASEAN country like Indonesia.

An Indonesia beset by prolonged civil unrest or weak government would thus be a minus for ASEAN. It could affect the standing of ASEAN and its effectiveness at a time of momentous changes and challenges in Southeast Asia and the Asia-Pacific. These include adjusting to the changing relations between the major powers, consolidating the ASEAN-10, adjusting to the requirements of the ASEAN Free Trade Area (AFTA), advancing confidence building and preventive diplomacy in the ASEAN Regional Forum, pushing Asia-Pacific regionalism through the Asia Pacific Economic Cooperation forum, and strengthening Asia-Europe dialogue and cooperation.

Compared with thirty years ago, Indonesia today is much more integrated with the international and regional economies. This has been happening both at the bilateral levels and, in the case of Southeast Asia, through sub-regional "growth triangles". Afta will further accelerate the process, while providing greater access to Southeast Asia's largest market. Any protracted instability in this vast country could affect this web of commerce and investments. If growth rates in Indonesia plummet as a result there could also be accelerated migration of people to neighbouring countries.

Note

This article first appeared in *ISEAS Trends*, June 1997.

6
Democratic Peace Theory and Asia: The Jury is Still Out

The merits of democracy as a system of government are obvious to democrats. Even if its shortcomings seem more obvious to non-democrats, objective and fair minded democrats would readily acknowledge them. But the relationship between democracy and interstate relations, especially on questions of war and peace, is more controversial even among democrats.

In academic circles, there are two broad intellectual traditions on the subject. The realist tradition argues that it is calculations of stark national interest that determine war and peace between states: systems of government are irrelevant. The liberal school on the other hand believes that systems of government do matter, and proponents of the liberal peace theory argue that liberal democracies do not go to war with each other. They cite empirical evidence in support of this claim, based on the study of international relations of liberal democracies in the past. There are eminent scholars in each camp.

Is there any merit in the claim that democracies do not go to war *with each other?* (Note the emphasis, because liberal democratic states do invade non-democratic states and tend to show strong distrust of powerful non-democratic countries.) Is there any basis for the claims of western leaders that making the world democratic would eliminate the scourge of war?

Stated baldly, without any qualifications, the claim that democracies do not go to war with each other is obviously simplistic. It is easy to see how democratically elected populist politicians in both India and Pakistan may exploit the mutually hostile sentiments of the two populations for political gain and in the process lead the two countries into war.

But does this really disprove the liberal peace theory? Here the definition of democracy becomes pertinent. After fifty years of clan and military regimes Pakistan has suddenly become a democratic polity since last year's elections. Also, while India is a democracy, it is a weak one. Mere elections do not a democracy make. Both Pakistan and India have serious deficiencies in the rule of law, which some would regard as one of the necessary conditions before a country can be considered a democracy.

The level of maturity of a democracy and its institutions is therefore an important factor and should not be dismissed lightly. Indeed some scholars have argued that the transition from dictatorships to democracy and the early phases of democratization may in fact witness more resort to war, because while authoritarian constraints on the free play of populist forces are no more, the habits and functioning institutions of a democracy are not yet in place.

Mature democracies would be those which have educated and well-informed publics schooled in the habits and responsibilities of a democracy. They are also likely to be countries of at least a fairly high level of economic and social development. Surely the way democracy functions in societies like Britain, Canada and Sweden, is quite different from the way it would function in India and Pakistan where nearly half the people (and a majority of the women) are illiterate and where mass poverty continues to exist.

The claim that mature democracies are highly unlikely to go to war against each other has at least *prima facie* validity. An examination of the state of relations between the democracies of Western Europe, between the US and Canada, and between Australia and New Zealand, would strongly suggest this. All are high income countries with an informed public opinion, a free press, a healthy civil society and the checks and balances of a democratic system.

The only slight doubt about this *prima facie* validity of the liberal peace theory as applied to the mature democracies is posed by an argument advanced by the realist theorists: that the benign state of affairs between mature democracies is due not to democracy as such but to the fact that for most of the time after World War Two these countries had a common enemy, in the absence of which, at some stage, nationalism will reassert itself. But this is left to be seen.

The liberal peace theory is still to be tested out in Asia. Some Western scholars have made a distinction between liberal and illiberal Asian democracies. In Asia, even the liberal ones tend to be either geographically non-contiguous or are not sufficiently mature to allow the liberal peace proposition to be tested. Only future history will tell, for instance, how relations between Korea and Japan will evolve.

But are North America and Western Europe unique, because of historical and cultural factors which are not easily replicated elsewhere? A healthy democracy entails both freedoms and responsibilities and a certain culture of give and take. It is easy to criticize, demonstrate, even riot. But it may not be so easy to acquire habits like respecting an opposing point of view, allowing public dissent, being civil and fair to a political opponent, refraining from the use of force or other undemocratic means to achieve political goals, and generally, respecting the political and civic rights of others as much as you would want them to respect your own.

Are these qualities unique to certain cultures? There are different views on this. But the democrats who say that they are not unique would point to the examples of countries like Germany and Japan, and argue that even where culture was once an impediment, it can change with the passage of time. The more sophisticated analysts will realize that while democratization can be sometimes gently prodded, it usually cannot be rushed or forced. It is usually better for it to grow naturally within the unique circumstances of each society in interaction with economic and other forces of change.

Note

This article first appeared in *ISEAS Trends*, June 1998.

7
ASEAN's Achievements are Endangered by Continuing Crisis

As foreign ministers of the Association of Southeast Asian Nations start their annual meeting in Manila today, their organization is facing a number of challenges. The most formidable is the economic crisis battering the region.

It used to be said that if economics went wrong in Southeast Asia, social and political instability would follow. This has already happened in Indonesia, the world's fourth-most populous nation and a key member of ASEAN. Political instability could spread if the crisis is prolonged, with the danger of exploitation by extremist elements.

Greater instability in domestic politics causes uncertainty, coloring the perceptions of foreign investors and financial markets, which tend not to differentiate among the individual countries of Southeast Asia.

The region's loss of international credibility is not entirely fair. Amid the publicity given to crony capitalism and corruption, it is easy to forget the achievements of ASEAN. Over the past thirty years it has kept the peace among its members, enabling them to concentrate on economic and social development. In so doing, ASEAN helped transform

Southeast Asia — once seen as the Balkans of Asia — from a region of poverty and almost endemic instability to one of relative peace and plenty.

This could not have happened without the support of the United States. But without the pragmatic, moderate and basically pro-Western leadership of the five founding members of ASEAN — Indonesia, Malaysia, the Philippines, Singapore and Thailand — Southeast Asia would have been a different and more troubled place.

ASEAN's reputation as a forward-looking organization of developing states was enhanced by its decision to establish the ASEAN Free Trade Area by 2003 and its role in nurturing Asia-Pacific regionalism, especially the ASEAN Regional Forum on security.

But ASEAN's achievements may be threatened if the region does not recover soon from the depression in Indonesia and worsening recessions in a number of other member states. The problem is how to implement far-reaching and potentially painful reforms amid deepening recession and growing social discontent — and when there is no indication how long the pain will have to be borne before recovery starts.

Recovery in the region is critically dependent on policies and developments in the major economic powers, over which ASEAN has no control.

Unlike Mexico's recovery from its financial crisis several years ago, Southeast Asia's revival is hampered by not only large private-sector debts, weaknesses in banking systems and depressed domestic demand, but also by continued exchange rate instability and the absence of a United States across the border to absorb more of the region's exports.

That is why a resurgence of growth in Japan and a strengthening of the Japanese yen against the dollar are imperative.

In this situation, the United States, as the world's major power, must provide leadership in devising and implementing strategies to help restore confidence in the region's markets and rekindle economic growth. Confidence is the key. The virtues that enabled ASEAN countries to register high growth rates in the past — hard work, high savings, investments in education and training, and mostly sound macroeconomic policies — remain in place.

If Southeast Asia fails to recover, the forces of political moderation and economic liberalization in the region could suffer setbacks. This would not be in the interests of either the West or Japan.

Note

This article first appeared in *International Herald Tribune*, 24 July 1998.

8
Surprising, Squabbling, Peaceful ASEAN

The picture of unity among the Association of Southeast Asian Nations (ASEAN) has been somewhat spoilt in recent months by bilateral spats between members.

Singapore and Malaysia argue over water, Malaysia offended Indonesia and the Philippines with the way its police expelled illegal Indonesian and Filipino migrants. Thailand and Myanmar continue to have border disputes.

Observers unacquainted with ASEAN ask if such public squabbling damages ASEAN. They are surprised when they find that the answer is: not much. Conceived in the throes of Cold War conflict, ASEAN has traditionally sought to avoid being held hostage to the bilateral quarrels of its members.

Rather, its attitude has been to seek and advance areas of common interest despite the existence of bilateral problems. Without this approach, the grouping of developing nations would not have been able to progress.

Consider for instance the fact that key members of ASEAN had been at war, near war or suffering from the trauma of separation (in the case of Singapore and Malaysia) only a few years before the organisation was established in 1967. It was necessary to stay clear of the legacy of bilateral bitterness and to focus instead on shared interests.

Bilateral problems between member states have occurred throughout ASEAN's history. They have included, just to mention a few, the Philippines-Malaysia dispute over Sabah; Indonesian claims to the Malaysian islands of Sipadan and Ligitan; the fracas between Singapore and the Philippines over the execution here of Filipina maid Flor Contemplacion; and the Malaysian-Singapore row over the state visit of Israeli president Herzog to Singapore.

These rows did not prevent ASEAN from making remarkable advances in regional cooperation and progressively enhancing its international stature from the mid-1970s to the mid-1990s.

Indeed, the regional framework provided by ASEAN with its vast networking and commitments through formal agreements and informal understandings in many areas has served to contain bilateral disputes.

The ASEAN financial and economic crisis in 1997–98 left in its wake economic wreckage and political instability. Indeed, the worst period in this respect was 1998–99 when several bilateral relationships were strained simultaneously — between Singapore and Malaysia and the Philippines.

Yet the numerous ASEAN meetings continued, not just with a "business as usual" attitude but with even more focus, in an effort to find a way out of the problems afflicting the members.

It was during these difficult years that ASEAN developed important new initiatives like the ASEAN Plus Three process involving the ASEAN countries together with China, Japan and South Korea. From 1999, it also focused attention on helping the four new ASEAN members — Cambodia, Laos, Myanmar and Vietnam — to integrate into the regional body.

Thus troubled bilateral relationships do not necessarily mean trouble across the board. Cooperation usually continues in other areas. The good relationship between the defence forces of Indonesia and Singapore has remained unaffected by the ups and downs in the political relationship since 1998. And behind the apparent tensions in Singapore-Malaysia relations, cooperation between police and intelligence services on crime and terrorism has continued.

However, if bilateral squabbles and the way they are handled have so far not been central to ASEAN's fortunes, they should not be viewed as irrelevant either. It cannot be denied that the quarrels of recent years, characterized as they sometimes have been by a certain stridency of nationalism and seeming carelessness about its possible consequences, did add to the adverse perceptions of ASEAN abroad.

Before the mid-1990s, when ASEAN basked in the glory of its achievements and its international stature, the 'cushion' that allowed it to get away with ill-managed bilateral quarrels was much bigger than it is today. ASEAN countries need to bear this in mind as the group seeks to recover its international credibility.

It should be borne in mind that although ASEAN as an organization has not wanted to be involved in the bilateral disputes of its members, it has from the beginning placed high premium on the need for members to resolve or manage them with care and sensitivity. Hence, more care given by members to the management of bilateral problems in accordance with the norms and spirit of ASEAN will not be amiss.

Note

This article was first published in *The Straits Times*, 16 September 2002. Reprinted with permission of The Straits Times © Singapore Press Holdings Limited.

9
Fast SARS Action Shows
ASEAN Not Just a Talk Shop

The star of the Association of Southeast Asian Nations (ASEAN) was dimmed in recent years by the Asian financial and economic crisis, the incorporation of the Indochina states and Myanmar as members, the political and economic problems of Indonesia, bilateral disputes, and diversion of foreign direct investment to China. Not a few observers dismissed the organization as an empty talk shop, long on words but very short on action. The nadir was probably reached around 1999–2000.

Since then, the war on terrorism and ASEAN's courtship by China and Japan with trade liberalization initiatives have improved the regional organisation's standing, but it has not recovered the position and prestige that it enjoyed a decade ago.

But ASEAN's response to the threat posed by Severe Acute Respiratory Syndrome (SARS) has a bounce and efficiency about it reminiscent of the good old days when the association was on a roll. At short notice, ASEAN was able to convene a meeting of the ASEAN health ministers, plus their counter-parts from China, Japan, and South Korea in Kuala Lumpur on 26 April, followed three days later by a special ASEAN leaders' meeting in Bangkok to address the SARS problem.

The meetings agreed on concrete measures to contain the spread of SARS, including the pre-departure screening of travelers and the sharing of information to trace people who may have come into contact with those already infected. There will be follow-up meetings of officials and experts and the setting up of an ad hoc ministerial-level task force to monitor enforcement of the decisions taken. Though implementation by some countries in some areas could initially be weak because of capacity inadequacies, there was no getting away from the sense of determination on the part of all members to get this right.

Even more significant was the special ASEAN-China leaders' meeting, which included Hongkong, held after the ASEAN summit on 29 April. SARS originated in China and China's posture of denial for the critical first few months after the outbreak was most unfortunate. If China had raised the alarm soon after the outbreak started, other countries in the region would have been better prepared to cope with the disease and may have suffered fewer infections and deaths. But governments in the region have been reluctant to criticise China publicly, believing it would be counterproductive. Nor is it in ASEAN's style to do so. Still, there was a need to send a message and to obtain Beijing's cooperation. What better way to do so than to invite it to a special summit with ASEAN leaders to discuss SARS? It was quintessential ASEAN behaviour.

China agreed to associate itself with the meeting's joint declaration of the ASEAN Leaders Meeting, which, apart from practical measures to check the spread of the disease across national borders, served to reinforce the need for transparency and regional and international cooperation, including working closely with the World Health Organization (WHO). "We have already learned our lesson", Chinese Premier Wen Jiabao was reported to have told a press conference at the end of the summit meeting, suggesting that the message had registered.

What accounted for the success of those hastily arranged meetings? The short answer is the strong shared economic interest among ASEAN countries to check the spread of SARS. A region that has experienced a series of blows starting with the Asian financial and economic crisis of 1997–98, cannot now allow itself to be brought down by a virus. Although SARS has so far generated a significant number of infections only in Singapore and Vietnam, tourism and associated service industries have already been badly hit across a large part of the region because tourists tend to view Southeast Asia or significant parts of it as a package destination.

In the past, shared fear has more than once driven ASEAN to greater cohesion. Could ASEAN's response to SARS be a sign of better times to come for the organization? As Singapore Prime Minister Goh Chok Tong said, the SARS affair may have strengthened the perception among foreign investors that they should not put all their eggs in one basket. Still, the objective economic and political circumstances of ASEAN have not changed significantly. But success can sometimes have its own dynamic and ASEAN successes at this juncture are most welcome. And perceptions matter a lot. Before 1997 favourable perceptions of ASEAN sometimes obscured its limitations. Post-1997, adverse perceptions often veil its continuing relevance and importance as a regional organization.

Whatever its shortcomings, ASEAN provides a framework for Southeast Asian countries to get together speedily to discuss matters of common concern. Its well established associate mechanisms, like the dialogue partnerships, also enable member countries, when necessary, to deal collectively, and with some strength, with major outside powers, instead of having to deal with them individually from a much weaker position. Without ASEAN, Southeast Asia could once again be the Balkans of Asia.

Note

This article was first published in *The Straits Times*, 7 May 2003. Reprinted with permission of The Straits Times © Singapore Press Holdings Limited.

PART II
Age of Terrorism, War in Iraq

10
The Changing Face of International Relations as America Combats Terrorism

There have been changes in American foreign policy since Sept 11.

Firstly, as Mr Fareed Zakaria, editor of *Newsweek* magazine has written, "a foreign policy of fiats and ultimatums will give way to one of negotiations and diplomacy", dictated by the need to obtain the cooperation of other countries to hold together the international coalition against terror.

Yet, beneath this new multilateralism, the vigour and tenacity of US demands on specific countries should not be underestimated. Further, the military part of the campaign against terrorism could be a multi-stage one, with Afghanistan only the first stage. If the US does not succeed in achieving its objectives through multinational cooperation, unilateral impulses could come to the fore again.

Secondly, the overriding priority being accorded to the anti-terrorism war means that certain countries and regions have become strategically more important. South Asia and Central Asia have acquired greater salience. In particular, there has been an about-turn in American policy on

Pakistan. Favours have to be returned and one can anticipate considerable economic support for Pakistan.

US support for Islamabad will probably not be at the expense of the partnership which the US has been forging with India in recent years. India is needed for the future geopolitical realities in Asia, centering on the rise of China.

Thirdly, as during the Cold War, military and security preoccupations could result in soft-peddling of concerns about human rights and democracy, which have featured prominently, even if selectively, in American foreign policy in the decade since the end of the Cold War. The degree of soft-peddling could vary, depending on the importance of particular countries to American interests.

The events since Sept 11 are also altering relations between the major powers. Perhaps the most intriguing is the closer relationship between Russia and the West arising from the common interest against terrorism. Such a development would be a setback to China's efforts to align itself with Russia in order to check dominant American power and obtain better leverage with Washington.

The common terrorist threat has contributed to a further improvement of Sino-US relations. China condemned the Sept 11 attacks on America. It is supporting American action against Afghanistan. Yet the strategic rivalry between the US and China in Asia is a long-term structural phenomenon related to the distribution of power in Asia, and will not just melt away. When the threat from international terrorism is contained, the rivalry could assume higher visibility again.

The war against terrorism has provided Japanese Prime Minister Junichiro Koizumi an opportunity to raise Japan's profile in international security affairs. A new legislation, pushed through Parliament will allow the Japanese military to provide logistical support to the US fleet in the Indian Ocean that is conducting military operations against Afghanistan.

What of Southeast Asia and ASEAN? The overall short-term effect is negative. The world economy has been adversely affected and Southeast Asian economies are suffering from the fallout. Economic pain provides fertile ground for extremist ideologies. However, the new security concerns give Asean a fresh opportunity to cooperate.

Archipelagic Southeast Asia will receive more attention from Washington because of its strategic sea lanes and the location of two major Muslim countries in the area. However, the attention will not always be of a welcome kind, given the inclination of the US since Sept 11 to view relations with other countries through the prism of the degree of support they offer in the anti-terror campaign.

The immediate effect of events since Sept 11 on individual Southeast Asian countries has varied. On Indonesia, it has been negative. The anti-US agitation by radical groups and the lack of firm action by the government, at least initially, have been blows to investor confidence. The US has promised Indonesia stronger economic support in return for cooperation in the fight against terrorism.

In Malaysia, despite a greater Islamic buzz, including more talk of an Islamic state, the net effect of the events since Sept 11 could be positive. The international campaign against terrorism would allow Prime Minister Mahathir Mohamad to take action against extremists with credibility and provide him with an opportunity to undercut moderate Malay support for Parti Islam SeMalaysia.

Philippine-US relations are set to strengthen: Manila will receive assistance from the US for the defeat of the Abu Sayyaf Group.

These may still be early days in the war against terrorism. One of the factors determining its duration and consequences would be whether the military campaign is extended to other countries, for instance Iraq. Another would be whether the terrorists are able to stage more catastrophic attacks against the US, especially attacks with radioactive or "dirty" nuclear devices.

A relatively benign outcome would help preserve US engagement in the world, and possibly also strengthen international institutions like the United Nations. On the other hand, an outcome which sees the US frustrated and damaged would be negative for the world, if it results in a reduced US involvement and leadership in world affairs.

Such an outcome could lead other major powers like Europe, China and Japan to play a larger role, but none would be able to substitute for the American role because of limitations peculiar to each.

Note

This article was first published in *The Straits Times*, 22 November 2001, under the title "Face of Future Global Ties as US Combats Terrorism". Reprinted with permission of The Straits Times © Singapore Press Holdings Limited.

11
There is Method to Howard's Madness

Australian Prime Minister John Howard's remark that Australia would be prepared to launch pre-emptive strikes against terrorists in other countries has predictably stirred a hornet's nest in Southeast Asia. Why did he make a remark which obviously was going to grate on Southeast Asian sensitivities?

One answer is domestic politics. He has been trying to demonstrate to Australians his strong leadership against terrorism, and this has gone down well with the Australian public.

Yet, the remark cannot be dismissed as a mere domestic political ploy. It was probably also meant to be a message to those countries, now or in the future, that might neither do enough to fight terrorists within their borders nor seek external assistance to strengthen their efforts.

It was also likely intended to score points with the United States by showing Australian solidarity with the US in the war against terrorism, especially with America's doctrine of pre-emptive strikes. It is interesting that, in contrast to the reactions from Southeast Asia, the US came out in support of Mr Howard's remarks — with support coming from the

White House itself. Although there is no direct evidence for it, it is possible that there is behind-the-scenes coordination between the US and Australia.

It is well known that the US expects its allies to help it carry the burden of international security in their regions. East Timor (Timor-Leste) was a good example of this: Australia carried the bulk of the burden, with the US providing logistic and valuable diplomatic support. Pre-emptive strikes against terrorists do not require large military forces, only small units of special forces with which Australia is well equipped.

Does this mean that such pre-emptive strikes are on the cards soon? Probably not. It should be noted that Howard's comments were qualified carefully: Only if there is no other alternative would pre-emptive action be considered.

After the Bali bombing, Indonesia is taking a firmer stance against terrorists and extremists in Indonesia. It would be foolish to make the domestic position of President Megawati Sukarnoputri more difficult by arousing a nationalist backlash. The Philippines is already cooperating well with the US to deal with the Abu Sayyaf Group, and new deployments of US troops are expected for another exercise with Philippine troops in the south of the country.

There have also been reports of possible new security cooperation between the Philippines and Australia. Meanwhile, Malaysia has both the will and relatively efficient security services to deal with terrorists.

If there is method in the apparent madness of Mr Howard's remarks, it is likely to be in the use of the spectre of pre-emptive action to prod Southeast Asian states to take firm action against terrorists, cooperate more effectively among themselves, and, where necessary, seek Australian or other external assistance to deal with the threat.

Many would, however, argue that the message could have been better put across privately to various governments. Perhaps. But there is sometimes merit in flying a kite in public, even engaging in a bit of sabre-rattling. It is a different way of putting across a message and conditioning thinking and expectations, even though some would refuse to credit Mr Howard with such sophistication.

Will the remarks damage Australia's relations with Southeast Asian states? In all likelihood, it is a passing storm, perhaps even a storm in a teacup. Southeast Asian leaders probably understand the game and there is already a close web of relations between Australia and a number of Southeast Asian countries. Public protestations do not always convey private thinking on complex matters of security, at least not all of it.

This, however, is not to suggest that pre-emptive strikes without at least the tacit consent of governments would be welcome.

Note

This article was first published in *The Straits Times*, 6 December 2002. Reprinted with permission of The Straits Times © Singapore Press Holdings Limited.

12
A Not So Happy New Year?

As one year is about to end and another begin, the outward calm of this holiday season belies uncertainty and unease. Religion-inspired terrorists, who would rather destroy the modern world as we know it if they cannot change it to one of their liking, are on the offensive from Bali to Mombassa. The spectre of war looms in the Middle East as Mr Saddam Hussein inclines towards a self-perceived heroic end by exacting maximum destruction on his foes, and, by extension, on his country.

Where Islamic terrorists and Mr Saddam's regime used to be as different as oil and water, each loathing the other, a war against Iraq could lead Al Qaeda to opportunistically step up its own attacks in order to tap into the Muslim sentiment aroused by the war.

Ironies and surprises come in quick succession. As Al Qaeda tries to dress its religious terrorist agenda in a pro-Palestinian, anti-Israel mantle in order to win over more Muslims for its war against "Jews and Crusaders", Mr Ariel Sharon in Israel seeks to tarnish Palestinians with the Al Qaeda brush.

The radical absolutists in the Muslim world are being matched in their anti-pluralist absolutism by sections of the Christian right in America. And to complicate an already dismal international situation, North Korea has chosen this moment, when America's attention is absorbed by Iraq and the war on terror, to embark on its own game of brinkmanship.

However, a conflict of civilizations is unlikely, given the moderate character of many Muslim regimes, and the common sense of much of the Muslim street, especially in Southeast Asia. After all, half of the world's Muslims live in South Asia, Bangladesh, India and Turkey, and they are less likely to heed the clarion call of the terrorist version of *jihad*.

In Singapore, most people are preoccupied with jobs, incomes and economy. All could be affected significantly by the events that will unfold over the next several months. Some intellectuals still debate the rights and wrongs of an American attack on Iraq, when the time for such debate is past. It is past because, unless Mr Saddam suddenly changes course (he is capable of near twelfth-hour about turns) or he is overthrown, war looks inevitable. More relevant at this stage would be discussion of the possible consequences of war, especially of what can go wrong.

A number of things can go wrong. One is the possibility of the use of weapons of mass destruction (WMDs), which many believe Iraq still possesses. Unlike the Gulf War of 1990–91, this time Mr Saddam may use chemical and biological weapons because his hold on power, even his life, are under threat.

There could also be adverse security and geostrategic consequences if a war against Iraq does not go well for the US. Any resulting strategic weakness of the US will embolden terrorist groups and rogue states. At this moment in history, the US occupies a pivotal position in the international security system. While many chafe at its perceived unilateralism and arrogance, there is as yet no other power that is in a position to assume its role as an anchor of international stability.

Nearer home, a US attack on Iraq will arouse Muslim sentiments in Southeast Asia. Most of the governments in the region will probably manage the situation relatively easily if the war is quick and decisive, though extremist groups in Indonesia may put the Jakarta government to sterner test.

Al Qaeda will have its own devilish designs, irrespective of any war against Iraq. One goal that it has indicated publicly is to deliver a blow to the US and western economies. It seems well aware of the developed world's economic vulnerabilities.

In Southeast Asia, Al Qaeda and its acolytes like the Jemaah Islamiyah may want to mount more attacks, possibly to coincide with a war on Iraq. Singapore is well protected by its efficient security services, but given its geographic location, no amount of controls and policing of borders can be fool-proof. The danger of terrorist attacks remains, especially if the terrorists go for progressively softer targets that are more difficult to secure.

The nightmarish possibilities outlined above may not all come to pass. The war against Mr Saddam may be won with relative ease. Or he may be overthrown even before an American-led attack begins. Either outcome in Iraq would likely have positive effects for the world.

The menace of international terrorism will then still remain. But the longer-term task of whittling down the terrorist infrastructure can proceed apace with increasing international cooperation and without possible setbacks flowing from a war gone wrong in Iraq.

What marks this period is its uncertainty, as we wait with abated breath for major events to unfold in the New Year. We hope that the outcome will be for the better, but we cannot be sure.

Note

This article was first published in *The Straits Times*, 2 December 2002. Reprinted with permission of The Straits Times © Singapore Press Holdings Limited.

13
Singapore's Stand on Iraq: Clear and Forthright

A friend asked me last week, before Foreign Minister S. Jayakumar's 14 March statement in Parliament, why Singapore had not taken a stand on Iraq. When I said, "on this, silence may be golden", he thought I was being facetious.

I explained that with the mounting anti-war tide, while it had been a season for posturing and grandstanding, it was also a time for sober reflection. It might be necessary sometimes to stake clear public positions quickly because of pressing domestic or international reasons, but should Singapore be rushed into taking a stand?

Unlike Britain, Australia or some countries in the Middle East, Singapore was providing neither combat troops nor attack bases. It has no direct political or economic interest in Iraq. As a small country, it could not afford to join the French game of trying to bring the American hyper-power down by a notch or two. Nor did Singapore have a restive Muslim majority to manage, as the leaders of Pakistan or Indonesia have, or a fundamentalist Islamic challenge as the Parti Islam SeMalaysia poses in Malaysia.

So if there were no compelling international or domestic reasons for it to rush to take a stand, I said, Singapore could take its time to do so. The political culture here is pragmatic, but on most issues of importance, the Government will eventually state its position, honestly and forthrightly.

But my interlocutor would not let me off the hook so easily. With debates raging in the world on issues like a possible American attack without United Nations authorization, and on the moral dimensions of the coming war, Singapore's silence seemed like a shirking of responsibility, he opined.

I tried to put across the complexities and misconceptions surrounding the Iraq issue. Was war as unambiguously immoral as some anti-war activists make it out to be? Ask the Kuwaitis who have experienced Iraqi invasion and a brutal occupation, or ask many ordinary Iraqis themselves. Or even ask the Iranians, whose country was also attacked by Iraqi President Saddam Hussein. There will be loss of civilian life during an American invasion, but these will probably be a fraction of the hundreds of thousands of his own countrymen that Mr Saddam has killed.

Will it be a violation of international law if war is waged without UN authorization? The UN is ideally the best way to go, but what can one say about it when, for twelve years, it has been unable to enforce its resolutions for Mr Saddam to disarm unconditionally?

But even many of American's allies in Europe are against the war, my friend interjected. Not quite correct, I had to admonish. The Iraq issue is indeed fracturing the Western alliance, and public opinion in many countries is against the war. But the leaders of Britain, Italy and Spain must have made calculations of their national interests, and they are not tiny states: The combined populations and gross domestic product of these three match those of Germany and France.

What of the Muslim world? By going to war against Mr Saddam, the United States is hardly going to war against Islam. Indeed, over the past decade, the US has fought two wars in the Balkans to protect Muslims from genocide by Christian authorities. Many Muslims may not see it that way because of their sense of fraternity with Muslims worldwide, especially those under attack from non-Muslims. Still, several Arab states have provided facilities to the US for the war against Iraq. The mood among most Arab governments by now must be one of resignation over something unavoidable, coupled with calculations of their interests in the post-war landscape. More may quietly assist the US to have the task finished quickly.

When it came out on 14 March, Professor Jayakumar's statement impressed my friend with its clarity and "boldness". There was no fudging, even in the dangerous times we live in. But while satisfied that a stand had at last been taken, my friend could not resist a last lunge. Was Singapore not too closely identified with the US, making us the odd man out in the region?

I acknowledged that Singapore's stated position on Iraq was different from its neighbours, especially Indonesia and Malaysia. Their national interests required different stances.

But in terms of overall bilateral ties with the US, Singapore was not as much an odd man out as it is sometimes made out to be. Singapore's neighbours have also been cooperating closely with Washington. Thailand and the Philippines have formal bilateral security treaties with the US, which Singapore does not. And Malaysia has had extensive military cooperation with the US for nearly two decades. Being the world' richest and strongest power, the US is sought after by many countries for trade, investments and security.

Singapore's stand is simple: International law and the credibility of the UN demand that Iraq disarm as required by various UN resolutions over the past twelve years. It has had more than enough time to do so. It was given a final chance under Security Council resolution 1441 of November 2002: disarm, or face the consequences. The consequences are now coming, with repercussions, for good or ill, on the Middle East and the rest of the world.

Note

This article was first published in *The Straits Times*, 18 March 2003. Reprinted with permission of The Straits Times © Singapore Press Holdings Limited.

14
Sept 11: Two Years On, Southeast Asia Breaks Terrorism's Deadly Lock

How has the war against terrorism in Southeast Asia fared in the two years since 9/11 and how well have states in the region responded to the challenge?

There have been some significant gains. The toppling of the Taleban regime in Afghanistan in the American-led military campaign was a clear plus. It meant radical groups could no longer send recruits for training in Afghanistan or use it as a sanctuary.

The arrests in Singapore and Malaysia since 2001 have crippled the Jemaah Islamiyah (JI) and Kumpulan Militan Malaysia (KMM) networks in the two countries. The remaining members are on the run, most having fled to other countries. Terrorist attacks in these two countries, especially on soft targets, can still happen, but it has become more difficult for JI to mount them or use these countries for transit or as bases.

There has been a significant change in Indonesia's attitude. Before the Bali bombing on 12 October last year, Indonesia was in a state of denial. Many Indonesians then saw the September 11 catastrophe as largely an American problem. Even after Bali attack, the feeling persisted for a few weeks among the public that elements of the Indonesian military or the American Central Intelligence Agency could have been behind the attack.

Over time, however, well-publicized investigations into the bombing and confessions of JI perpetrators convinced Indonesians that they had a genuine terrorist problem on their hands. There have been dozens terrorists arrested since then, including some connected with the JW Marriott Hotel bombing last month.

Thailand, on its part, has taken a more proactive stance since May this year to deal with terrorists on its soil. It has made a number of arrests, including that of JI operational leader Hambali.

Another legacy of September 11 is that there has been intensified cooperation at the bilateral, regional and international levels to fight terrorism, including stepped up bilateral intelligence exchanges. The ASEAN Ministerial Committee on Transnational Crime has been a useful platform to share best practices in the fight against terrorism. International bodies like the United Nations Security Council's Counter-Terrorism Committee (CTC) and the Financial Action Task Force now require countries to report regularly their progress in specific areas of the global anti-terror war.

Despite all these gains, much still needs to be done. It is the political will and capacity of individual countries to act against terrorist cells within their own borders and establish and enforce the necessary laws and regulations that count most. Exchange of intelligence makes little practical difference on the battlefield if it is not acted upon. Impressive multilateral workshops and training modules do not enhance the capacity of a country to fight terrorism if what is learned is not translated into practical application.

The political will and capacities vary from country to country. Singapore and Malaysia can be said to have unambiguously demonstrated both the will and the capacity to fight terrorism. The picture in the other key countries is more mixed.

Indonesia is still reluctant to embark on a comprehensive crackdown on the JI within its borders, preferring instead to act mostly against that part of the network responsible for the Bali bombings, and, presumably, the JW Marriott Hotel bombing in Jakarta. The clandestine JI network in Indonesia is still extensive, with hundreds of members, and with links to other radical Muslim groups that operate openly. The recent arrests have probably only scratched the surface. Indonesia has a considerable way to go to develop proper legal and judicial systems and to build the capacity to act effectively on matters like border controls and terrorist financing.

However, perhaps it is better to count the blessings than to bemoan what has not been possible thus far. It is not difficult to understand the Indonesian dilemma. Islam is a significant force in the democratic politics of the country and, in view of the approach of elections next year, political leaders have to tread gingerly against the JI so as not to invite a backlash from conservative Muslims.

Another country that has been an important link in the terrorist network in Southeast Asia is the Philippines. It was the first Southeast Asian country into which Al Qaeda moved to co-opt local Muslim groups into its global jihad against the West. Thus the Abu Sayyaf Group (ASG) and the Moro Islamic Liberation Front have been linked with Al Qaeda from the early and mid-1990s and some Southeast Asian JI operatives have been trained in MILF camps.

On the surface at least, the Philippines has the will to combat terrorism and has shown willingness to seek American assistance to fight the ASG. However the anti-terrorism war is hampered by capacity shortcomings and lack of a coherent and effective strategy to deal with the MILF, the more formidable of the two main rebel groups. Unless the MILF can be made to disassociate itself from JI and Al Qaeda, the Philippines will remain a weak link in the war against terrorism because MILF controlled areas of the country can provide sanctuary and training facilities for Southeast Asian terrorist elements.

The problems for the Philippine government are compounded by weak governance, reported corruption in the military, and factionalism in the MILF, with the more radical elements wanting to keep up the armed struggle and links with foreign terrorist groups.

Thailand too has an important role to play in the region's war against terrorism. This predominantly Buddhist land has been used by Al Qaeda agents and JI terrorists not only for transit but also as a meeting place and hide-out. Hambali, for instance, was hiding in Thailand when he was arrested last month.

Thailand's graduation from denial to cautious acknowledgment of a terrorist problem, has been followed by some arrests of JI suspects. Still, the country has been proceeding very cautiously, apparently so as not to scare off tourists or alienate the Muslim population in the south.

So some doubts remain about whether Bangkok is fully on board the drive against terrorism in Southeast Asia.

JI has tried to infiltrate Muslim communities in other parts of the region, especially those that feel marginalized or persecuted, for instance the Cham Muslim community in Cambodia and the Rohingya community in Myanmar's western Rakhin state. Hence the need for vigilance against a nimble adversary ever prepared to use any opportunity to advance its cause.

In conclusion, while terrorism in Southeast Asia has suffered setbacks over the past two years, it remains a threat. Terrorists are unlikely to be able to overthrow or endanger the survival of any government, but they do have the capacity to inflict serious economic harm by damaging investor sentiment and the tourism industry.

Radical Islam in Southeast Asia still has little influence in the mainstream of Southeast Asian societies. So long as the terrorists have not acquired a critical mass and deep roots in mainstream local societies they can be isolated and hunted down if countries of the region can marshal the will and capacity to take effective action.

The future fortunes of JI, for better or worse, are also likely to be affected by developments outside the region. What happens to Al Qaeda on the global stage and what happens in Islam in countries like Saudi Arabia and Iran could have an important bearing. Needless to say, so will the eventual outcome of the struggle now shaping up in Iraq, which is drawing radical groups from Iraq's neighbouring countries, and its impact on America's global policies and posture.

ASEAN countries are fighting terrorism not to please the Americans. They have powerful reasons of their own to do so. The radical agenda terrorist groups espouse and their violent methods are unacceptable not only to the governments but to the vast majority of the people of Southeast Asia.

Note

This article was first published in *The Straits Times*, 11 September 2003. Reprinted with permission of The Straits Times © Singapore Press Holdings Limited.

15
US Bungling Makes Iraq a Problem for the World

It is plain for all to see that America's Iraq war has not gone the way the White House had expected.

The political fall out from the failure to find any weapons of mass destruction (WMD) may in the end prove to be the lesser of the headaches for the United States. The Bush Administration probably believed, when it went to war, that Saddam Hussein must have hidden his WMD, not an unreasonable assumption in view of the Iraqi leader's character.

However, the war was not just about WMD, though that was easier to sell to the US public. It was also supposed to change the strategic landscape in the Middle East by building in Iraq a model for the region.

On hindsight, these were audaciously ambitious, even utopian goals. In the debates preceding the war, there were some sober and respected voices who questioned the wisdom of America' course. They did produce a certain unease in me at the time about whether the old and new conservatives in the Bush regime had really got it right.

However, I dismissed these qualms in the belief that the US Administration probably knew best, since it had many clever people with access to a wide array of intelligence. Surely, I thought, America would have learnt from the

Vietnam experience, where the "best and brightest" had also misjudged the enormity of the tasks they would face. Alas, it turns out that a new generation has to relearn the same lessons, even if Iraq's parallels with Vietnam should not be overdrawn.

Now the US has to fight a guerilla war it did not expect and was not prepared for. If it had been anticipated, the calculus of loss and gain could well have dictated a different course from the outset.

It is not easy for a conventional army to shift to counter-insurgency warfare in an alien country. It is especially difficult for the American army to do so because it has no recent experience or expertise in counter-insurgency. Guerillas in the region cannot be defeated without good tactical human intelligence and the requisite Arab-language capabilities that go with that.

But Iraq is no longer just an American burden; it has become a problem for the world. A war that was meant to weaken radicalism and deliver a blow to international terrorism appears, at least for now, to have given a boost to both. Though supporters of the old regime still form the bulk of the resistance in Iraq, Islamic radicals from the surrounding region, including some linked to Al Qaeda, have been pouring in to fight Americans.

This is a pity because Al Qaeda was otherwise suffering setbacks in Afghanistan, Pakistan, Southeast Asia and in Saudi Arabia. But now it is likely to get many more recruits for its cause.

The US is not waging a war against Islam, but the invasion of Iraq appears to have given wide currency to the belief in Muslim countries that it is. TV images of the apparent ease with which US military men and machines have been targeted make the US look vulnerable, lifting the morale and firing the zeal of jihadists. There is also the danger of Iraq becoming a crucible for turning out thousands of new battle-hardened jihadists who will want to destabilise their own societies when they return from Iraq.

Thus, radicalism and terrorism worldwide, including in Southeast Asia, are likely to get a boost if the situation in Iraq is not brought under control. A chilling reminder of the continuing threat that terrorism poses can be found in a United Nations report released on 1 Dec. It said Al-Qaeda's ideology has continued to spread, and about the only thing stopping terrorists from conducting attacks with chemical, biological or "dirty" radiation bombs is lack of technical expertise, which they will try to acquire.

The situation in Iraq, while serious, can still be managed if the US, Europe and the UN can agree on a common international effort. But if the US has to slog on for years largely on its own, the diversion of its energy and resources to the Middle East could have significant strategic implications for the Asia-Pacific. It could mean, for instance, greater US dependence on other Asian powers for managing Asian security, resulting in acceleration in the geopolitical rise or revival of powers like China, Japan and India.

Note

This article was first published in *The Straits Times*, 11 December 2003, under the title "Why Iraq is Not Just America's Problem". Reprinted with permission of The Straits Times © Singapore Press Holdings Limited.

16
Iraq is Not Like Vietnam — For Now

Is Iraq turning into a Vietnam?

Consider: Optimism among American official circles about the progress of the Vietnam war was shattered by the Vietcong uprising in South Vietnam in February 1968. The Tet (Lunar New Year) offensive was timed for an American presidential election year and, though widely regarded as a military failure, had the intended political effects.

Then-president Lyndon B. Johnson declared that he would not seek re-election for a second term, ordered the suspension of bombing on large parts of North Vietnam and made overtures for a negotiated settlement of the war. Presidential candidate Richard Nixon, who eventually won the election, made it his campaign platform to end the war and bring American troops home, albeit on honourable terms. These developments signalled that America had decided it could not win the war; the only question that remained was the terms of the retreat.

The year 2004 is also proving to be a year in which violence is increasingly being used by various groups to achieve political ends. Those who carried out the deadly Madrid bombings on the eve of the Spanish elections, succeeded in bringing to power a government opposed to the Spanish military involvement in Iraq. It is said to have been offered a "truce" from further attacks, if Spain withdraws its troops from Iraq. A foiled follow-up attempt to attack a high speed train track was probably intended to reinforce the message, if it had succeeded. There have been threats against Japanese interests, and Japanese civilians have been seized as hostages by unidentified groups in Iraq. And there are likely to be more pressures on countries which are helping to stabilize Iraq with troop contributions.

Are we going to see a repeat of 1968 in the security situation in Iraq and its impact on American policies to Iraq? Probably not, and at least not so soon or in the same way. On the surface, recent events in Fallujah in the Sunni triangle and the outbreak of pockets of Shi'ite insurgency in southern Iraq bear similarity to 1968 Vietnam. The appearance of progress in subduing the Sunni insurgency and of relatively confident movement towards Iraqi self-rule has been dealt a blow, and in an American presidential election year. TV images of the battle for Fallujah bear some resemblance to US Marines struggling to retake Hue from the communist forces in 1968.

However, at this stage, it is still not clear how much of a turning point the present events in Iraq constitute. Much would depend on how strong the insurgency in the so-called Sunni triangle proves to be and on whether the Shi'ite insurgency in the south can be confined to a minority of the Shi'ite population who have been supporters of radical cleric Moqtada al-Sadar, and can be ended quickly.

Until the recent events, coalition forces seemed to have the insurgency in the Sunni triangle fairly well under control. The insurgency is unlikely to have suddenly become much stronger and better organized. The killing, mutilation and grotesque display before television cameras of the four American security contractors was reminiscent more of Mogadishu 1993 and may have been calculated to have the same effect on American public opinion and government policy. The coalition authorities obviously could not allow this to go unpunished. Yet the danger is that the heavy handed military response, that has apparently caused many civilian Iraqi casualties, could incite more Iraqis to join the insurgents. In counter-insurgency warfare political considerations must remain paramount; wherever possible a scalpel should be used to weed out the undesirables instead of a sledgehammer which also hits many innocent bystanders.

The Shi'ite insurgency is potentially the more dangerous one because Shi'ites form the majority of the population of Iraq. So far there is not enough indication that this insurgency will spread to the majority of the Shi'ites. It may not be in the interest of Grand Ayatollah Ali al-Sistani, who is said to command much wider support among the Shi'ites than Mr Al-Sadar, to see that happen. A good deal will therefore depend on whether he remains willing and able to cooperate with the coalition to keep the Shi'ite south of the country relatively quiet.

Perhaps most importantly, unlike Vietnam after Tet in 1968, there are no serious divisions at present among the political elite in America, including Congress, on the need to stay the course in Iraq, though there is likely to be growing debate on the methods of achieving America's goals there. The prospect of an Iraq in chaos or under a radical anti-Western regime is viewed as just too serious a threat to American security and its vital interests in the Gulf region. The majority of American public opinion at this point remains behind the Administration. And most of America's allies are still standing firm against pressures from radicals within and outside Iraq.

Still, the latest developments in Iraq cannot be treated lightly. They indicate that the insurgency could become more serious, especially if the American-dominated coalition authority continues to display political ineptitude in handling it. The spectre of a disastrous and widespread revolt involving both Sunni and Shi'ite Iraq or a civil war looms larger than ever before. As American casualties increase, and unease about the war grows in this election year, fuelled also by the hearings in Washington on the 9/11 event, public support for it may decline.

If the situation continues to deteriorate, America will have to make compromises on its goals in Iraq and the Middle East, to avoid the worst case scenarios. If America could start a new relationship with China in the early 1970s to prepare for an exit from Vietnam, could it not have a new opening to countries like Iran and Syria and a new approach to Arab and European allies for the stabilization of Iraq? But the price, among others, will probably have to include a just settlement of the Israeli-Palestinian dispute.

Note

This article was first published in *The Straits Times*, 13 April 2004. Reprinted with permission of The Straits Times © Singapore Press Holdings Limited.

17
Losers and Winners in the Iraq War

The Americans probably never expected things to turn out this way: among the external actors, the biggest loser of the Iraq war so far has been the United States.

US standing in the world, especially in the Arab/Muslim world, has been damaged. Its policies in Iraq and the Middle East are perceived as unilateral and unwise, betraying poor understanding of the problems and an over-emphasis on military/security instruments. Growing instability in Iraq and rising anti-Americanism in the Arab and Muslim world are combining to produce unease even among America's friends and allies.

Pro-American Arab regimes find themselves under pressure as radical groups, including Al Qaeda, try to turn the tide of anti-American feeling — fuelled by developments in Iraq and by America's perceived support of Israel — against them. The grand American scheme for reform in the Middle East — the Greater Middle East Initiative — looks doomed. It has become politically perilous for Arab leaders to embrace such an openly made-in-America project.

On the US domestic front, questions multiply about the way Iraq has been handled. If more bad news keeps on coming out of Iraq, President Bush's re-election prospects in November could be affected.

The Iraq war has also stretched American military forces. Given the demands on the military of the conflict in Afghanistan and the war against terrorism, the US cannot afford to fight another significant war without major increases in military manpower and defence expenditures, with their attendant economic and political costs.

Arguably the biggest and most obvious gainers of the Iraq imbroglio so far have been Islamic radicalism and terrorism, both of which have received a significant boost. In Iraq the terrorists have found a new ground for breeding radical Muslims and turning out a new generation of jihadists. Al Qaeda web-sites have, since the outbreak of the Iraq war, been urging Muslims to go to Iraq to fight the Americans. Most of those who have heeded this call so far are from Arab countries near Iraq and from Western Europe.

Al Qaeda-linked and other radical groups have also begun to use terrorist outrages to pressurise states with troops in Iraq to withdraw them. The Madrid bombings in late March 2004 illustrate this. We can expect more terrorist outrages aimed at getting more countries to withdraw their troops from Iraq.

Less obviously, major Asian powers are proving to be strategic beneficiaries of the Iraq war. America's preoccupation with Iraq and the war against terrorism has given China more space and elbow room to pursue its interests in the Asia-Pacific. China has been diplomatically active in Asia, pursuing its strategic interests through initiatives like the proposal for a free trade area with ASEAN. However, China's satisfaction with this state of affairs could be tempered by concerns about potential instability in the

Gulf region if Iraq cannot be stabilised, given China's growing need for imported energy.

Japan has been provided a new opportunity to raise its international security profile by sending troops to help reconstruct Iraq — the first time it has done so to a country where there is ongoing conflict. However, Prime Minister Koizumi's plan to move Japan towards becoming a more "normal" power could suffer a setback if terrorist attacks on Japanese interests, at home or abroad, make the Japanese public demand a withdrawal of its troops. He would then have to mediate between Japanese domestic opinion and the vital strategic interests and role of the US, its only ally and security guarantor.

India has benefited from America's war on terrorism and its preoccupation with the Middle East and Afghanistan, which together have led to a more friendly Pakistani posture towards India. Also, as the largest Indian Ocean littoral state and a rising power with naval potential, India has become strategically more important to the US, raising prospects for closer strategic cooperation between the two countries. However any outcome in Iraq which further strengthens Islamic radicalism would obviously be against Indian interests.

Finally the Iraq war has had some beneficial impact on efforts to curb nuclear proliferation. The application of the Bush Administration's doctrine of pre-emption to Iraq could have been a factor in the breakthrough in the long running negotiations with Libya to end its development of weapons of mass destruction.

More important, the rest of the world, in particular the United Nations and the leading nations of the European Union, alarmed by the prospect of US unilateralism and pre-emptive strikes, have redoubled their efforts to ensure that Iran does not produce nuclear weapons. On the whole, there is now better international cooperation to prevent nuclear proliferation, spurred also by the more recent revelations of the proliferation activities of Pakistani scientist Abdul Qadeer Khan.

Note

This article was first published in *The Straits Times*, 14 May 2004. Reprinted with permission of The Straits Times © Singapore Press Holdings Limited.

18
Is Bangladesh Waking Up to Danger of Islamic Militancy?

Over the past few years there have been troubling reports about the growth of Islamic militancy in Bangladesh, which has received a lot of play in the press. For example, the grenade attacks against leaders of the main opposition party, the Awami League (AL), including one in January 2005 that killed former finance minister Shah Kibria, have been well publicized. So too have reports of isolated attacks on members of the Hindu minority as well as pressures on the Ahmadi minority.

For a number of years, however, the government led by the Bangladesh Nationalist Party (BNP) seems to have been in a state of denial over these developments, prompting observers to draw parallels with the attitude of the Indonesian government to the activities of the Jemaah Islamiyah in Indonesia before the Bali bombings.

But now some change seems to be in the air. Analysts believe this has been prompted by renewed pressure on the Dhaka government from the international community — aid donors in particular — to take action against terrorist elements in the country. Some media have even called the tougher stance as a "crackdown" — with the government reportedly banning radical organizations such as the Jammat-ul-Mujahideen, among others, and making some arrests, though the authorities have been careful to dress these up as law and order initiatives.

While this apparent change in attitude is heartening, there are also signs of a certain defensiveness and internal differences in the government, leading to speculation that the presence of fundamentalist Islamic parties in the ruling coalition government may be making it difficult to take strong and sustained action against the militants.

Since it came to power in 2001, the ruling coalition government led by the BNP under the leadership of Begum Khaleda Zia has had two Islamic fundamentalist parties among its coalition partners. First, the long established Jamaat-e-Islami (JEI) which has seventeen out of 300 elected MPs and two ministerial posts; and the smaller Islamic Oikyo Jote (IOJ) with two MPs.

Some observers are not perturbed by the presence of the JEI in the government, arguing that the JEI has only a small popular support base and its participation in the ruling coalition helps moderate its politics. However, other analysts view its role in the government in a dismal light. They say that while it projects itself as a responsible coalition member, JEI's position in the government provides encouragement, even a degree of protection, to the radicalization efforts of various militant groups operating in the country. As has been noted widely, there are also personal ties between some JEI and IOJ officials, on the one hand, and radical organisations operating at the grass roots level, on the other.

Perhaps benign neglect or wishful thinking explain the government's past reluctance to crack down on radical elements and apprehend those who perpetrate the kind of violence that led to the death of former finance minister Kibria.

The problem of Islamic radicalism in Bangladesh is also interwoven with the bitter polarization in its domestic politics between the two main political parties — the BNP and the AL — and with the country's relations with India.

According to some analysts, the BNP needs the coalition with the fundamentalist parties as a counter to the AL and, possibly, India, which is perceived as supporting the AL. A measure of Islamic fervour on the ground, even if radical in orientation, may be seen to serve a similar purpose. It would be in the ideological and practical interest of the radicals to attack the secular AL to weaken it.

If the BNP government does operate on these premises and views the militants as a useful attack cavalry against its domestic political enemies, it would be very difficult to crack down on militancy. But this would be seriously short-sighted of the government, considering how dependent the country is on foreign investments and aid, which could dry up if Bangladesh is perceived to be a hot-bed of Islamic terrorism.

Popular support for the fundamentalists is not high and neither the JEI nor any other radical group has any chance of coming to power through the ballot box. Mainstream Islam in the country has a tradition of moderation, with marked humanist and Sufi influences, and Bangladeshis generally find the austere demands of fundamentalist Islam unappealing. A significant secular, liberal intellectual tradition also exists, which the educated elite still value, even if it has been put on the defensive by the rising extremism. So there is hope yet.

Note

This article was first published in *The Straits Times*, 7 April 2005, under the title "Dhaka Wakes Up to Danger of Islamic Militancy". Reprinted with permission of The Straits Times © Singapore Press Holdings Limited.

19
Pakistan Faces a Gathering Storm

Since 9/11 Pakistan has become so much a part of the global security grid that adverse developments there can send shock waves through the international system. Sadly, this proud and attractive country with much potential has become one of the main centres of international terrorism and extremism and has been drifting towards increased instability. There are no easy options available to arrest these trends.

Much of the remnants of Al Qaeda, including Osama bin Laden and his deputy Ayman al-Zawahiri, are believed to be hiding in the remote tribal areas of Pakistan where they have established a safe haven. They are reported to have regrouped, become stronger and acquired greater ability to plan attacks against targets abroad than anytime since 2001. There are also a host of home-grown Pakistani extremist Islamic organizations, some of which, used in the past by the Pakistani state to fight the Indians in Kashmir, have now turned against their patron. Further, the Pashtun belt of Pakistan is widely believed to be a base area for the recruitment and training of neo-Taleban fighters waging war against NATO forces and the government of President Hamid Karzai across the border in Afghanistan. As NATO forces incur more casualties in Afghanistan at the hands of the neo-Taleban, pressure seems to be mounting in Washington for some kind of action against the sanctuaries in Pakistan. Meanwhile anti-Americanism has grown and support for President Pervez Musharraf among the people has plummeted.

The Pakistani state's writ in the tribal areas, weak even in better times, has deteriorated. The bloody Lal Masjid (Red Mosque) affair showed the confidence and willingness of the militants to take on the state even in the capital Islamabad. Its aftermath has been marked by increased unrest in the Pashtun belt and a spate of suicide bombings in the country. An embattled President Musharraf has vowed to take on and destroy the monster of extremism in the country. But is he really able to do so after it has grown to such proportions?

How has Pakistan allowed itself to become a hotbed of terrorism and extremism, even though, in the overall population of the country, the extremists remain a minority?

Part of the answer lies in the proxy war waged by America, Pakistan and Saudi Arabia in the 1980s against the Soviets in Afghanistan by recruiting, training and supporting scores of thousands of Muslim holy warriors for that conflict. In those days, Islamic extremism was seen as a worthy and potent weapon against godless communism. Pakistan was an active and keen participant in that enterprise because the presence on its western border of the army of the Soviet Union, then seen to be allied to Pakistan's bitter adversary on its east, India, was an anathema to Islamabad.

However, it is not the whole answer. Another important dimension is that the Pakistani state, and in particular the military and the Inter Services Intelligence, has a history of riding the tiger of extremism to advance the state's domestic and external political interests, especially since the time of President Zia ul-Haq. This has been well documented, including by Pakistani writers (see for instance Husain Haqqani's book *Pakistan: Between Mosque and Military*). In addition to the anti-Soviet crusade in Afghanistan, such a policy could be seen in helping the Taleban, many recruited from the madrasahs of the Pashtun belt in Pakistan, to come to power in Afghanistan in the post-Soviet phase and in the support for Pakistan-based jihadi groups engaged in the insurgency in the Indian part of Kashmir. The enmity with India could have been an important motivation behind these policies: externally, they have been seen as suitable ripostes to perceived Indian designs in the neighbourhood of Pakistan while internally they served to reinforce Pakistan's separate Islamic identity. Now the tiger looks more ferocious while the state looks more frayed and weaker than before. That this increasingly troubled state also possesses nuclear weapons naturally conjures up nightmarish scenarios in the international community.

Is the state now able to dismount from the tiger and take decisive action against Al Qaeda and other extremists? At stake is nothing less than peace and stability in Pakistan which is a prerequisite for the economic progress that the Pakistani people aspire to. At stake also is regional stability in South Asia as well as the international struggle against terrorism. In this globalized world success enjoyed by extremists in one country encourages extremists elsewhere. It may be recalled that before 9/11 Southeast Asian extremists had significant links with like-minded groups in Pakistan and Afghanistan and these links could revive if terrorism and extremism continue to grow in the Pakistan-Afghanistan region.

To decisively confront domestic extremists, a serious break from the past is needed. This would include further reductions of tensions with India, if only to release more troops from the contingency of conflict with India to deployment in the tribal areas. Much of the Pakistani army today is trained and deployed for conventional conflict with India, not for counter-insurgency. It would also need a more effective government which enjoys better support from the majority of people who constitute the moderate segments of society. Given the entrenched position of the military in Pakistan over many years and their particular mindset on what is good for the country, given the weaknesses of the moderate civilian political parties and the polarizations in society over the years, there seems to be no easy way out of the quandary that Pakistan currently faces.

Note

This article was first published in *The Business Times*, 3 August 2007.

20
Southeast Asia Succeeds in Keeping Terrorism at Bay

Seven years after the 9/11 attacks, the war on terrorism continues, with no end in sight.

In a recent survey of Al Qaeda, *The Economist* called America's war on terror "inconclusive". The terrorist threat, it said, will last many more years. It derives currently mostly from "ungoverned, undergoverned and ungovernable" areas of the Muslim world and the "virtual caliphate" of cyberspace.

Yet apart from a mention of "the chain of islands between Indonesia and the Philippines" in its list of poorly governed lands, the article barely touches on Southeast Asia — once trumpeted as the "second front in the war against terrorism".

In fact, Southeast Asia has had important successes in the fight against terrorism. The threat has by no means been eliminated. But it has been reduced compared with its peak in 2001–2002. The networks of the main terrorist organization in Southeast Asia, the Jemaah Islamiyah (JI), have been virtually destroyed in Singapore and Malaysia. JI has also been weakened in Indonesia, its main base. The Philippines has had success against the terrorist-cum-bandit Abu Sayyaf Group (ASG).

What accounts for these Southeast Asian successes? First, no country affected by terrorism is now in a state of denial, though Indonesia and Thailand were so in the first couple of years after 9/11. Since 2003–2004 all affected countries have taken the threat seriously.

Second, the region's security services — especially those of Malaysia and Singapore (notwithstanding Mas Selamat Kastari's escape) and the counter-terrorism units of the Indonesian national police — have been effective and professional. They have based their efforts on the effective use of intelligence, relying as far as possible on the police as the front-line force. In the southern Philippines where counter-insurgency operations require the use of military units, excessive use of force such as aerial bombings has been avoided.

Third, there has been intelligence cooperation among ASEAN countries as well as between them and the intelligence services of friendly powers such as the United States and Australia. Such cooperation has resulted in the capture of important terrorists, including Hambali, the operational head of JI, in Thailand in 2004. Leads provided by Singapore led to the recent arrests of JI elements near Palembang, Sumatra and the seizure of bombs and explosives by the Indonesian police.

ASEAN states have not been shy about seeking foreign assistance too. The Australian police have worked closely with the Indonesian police to investigate terrorist bombings, and US special forces have provided technical intelligence and operational advice to the Philippines military. Since front-line operations have all been conducted by the local security forces, Western agencies have left only a very small footprint.

Another factor in Southeast Asia's success is the lack of sanctuaries for terrorists, of the kind that Al Qaeda and the Taleban enjoy in Pakistan. Though parts of southern Philippines remain poorly governed, ASG and JI terrorists there have been kept on the run.

Southeast Asian Muslims seem less receptive to extremist Islamic ideas than Arab or South Asian Muslims. It has been said that Islam became softer as it moved eastwards from the Arabian peninsula. By and large this remains the case, especially in Indonesia, the world's largest Muslim-majority country, notwithstanding the recent conservative turn there.

ASEAN governments have also given militants less room for manoeuvre by settling or defusing local conflicts. This is important because radicals can exploit local conflicts to advance their cause. Al Qaeda tried to enlist Muslim separatist rebellions and the JI has sought to exploit sectarian conflict within Indonesia. Jakarta recently settled the long-running Aceh conflict as well as the sectarian conflicts in the Moluccas and central Sulawesi. The Philippines government has sought a negotiated end to the rebellion by the Moro Islamic Liberation Front (MILF).

Despite these successes, there is much left to be done. Extremist groups are still active in Indonesia. JI elements need to be separated from the MILF in the Philippines. State capacity needs to be extended to poorly governed regions. And extremist ideology needs to be discredited, something which can be done effectively only by esteemed Muslim religious scholars and community leaders.

Note

This article was first published in *The Straits Times*, 4 August 2008, under the title "ASEAN Succeeds in Keeping Terrorism at Bay". Reprinted with permission of The Straits Times © Singapore Press Holdings Limited.

PART III

The Big Boys of Asian Geopolitics

21
China Needs to Act Like a Good Neighbour

Because of its size, proximity and potential power, China can easily arouse unease among many of its Southeast Asian neighbours.

Such apprehension is often compounded by latent resentment in the region at the dominant role of local ethnic Chinese in commerce and memories of Beijing's support for revolutionary communism in these countries during the Cold War.

China needs to act as a model good neighbour to allay suspicions and build confidence. Yet to many Southeast Asians it seems to be doing the opposite in the South China Sea. The recent incidents involving China and the Philippines in the vicinity of the Mischief Reef in the disputed Spratly Islands are the latest manifestation of this.

Even though some other claimants to the Spratlys have been consolidating their presence, the spectacle of a permanent member of the United Nations Security Council and a potential super-power planting territorial markers and building occupation structures on reefs in new areas also claimed by the Philippines, which is a far smaller and weaker country that China, is a troubling one.

Beijing has said it does not want to deal with the South China Sea dispute in the eighteen nation ASEAN Regional Forum set up to handle just this kind of issue. It prefers instead to deal one by one with its much smaller neighbours. Such behavior makes it difficult to accept at face value China's ritual assurances that its intentions in the region are benign.

There is much concern in Southeast Asia about the extent of Beijing's claims to the South China Sea itself, as distinct from the Spratlys and other disputed groups of islands and reefs.

Do the Chinese maps showing a broken line encompassing much of the South China Sea define the country's territorial waters, as many believe? The tongue-shaped claim, based on some vague historical consideration, is baffling to Southeast Asians.

Beijing's claim is also ominous because it overlaps territorial claims, exclusive economic zones and continental shelves of Southeast Asian states. If accepted as valid, it would turn much of the South China Sea, through which vital trade routes pass, into China's territorial waters and bring the maritime boundaries of China into the heart of Southeast Asia.

The motives behind Beijing's claim are unclear. Some observers point to the resources of the sea and seabed. On the threshold of the 21st century, a quest for territory to obtain resources seems a singularly old-fashioned route to economic power.

Resource-poor countries like Japan, South Korea and Singapore have shown that modern economic strength comes from skills, organization and technology combined with the ability to trade.

Another motive sometimes ascribed to China's actions is to assert control of the South China Sea as a lever to attain strategic dominance in Southeast Asia. If so, both the means and the end are likely to be contested by other major powers who will view them as cutting across their vital interests. Surely China must know this.

Or is it engaged in a preemptive move to prevent some potential rival from seeking to dominate Southeast Asia in future, thereby threatening China's southern flanks? But a quest for security which produces insecurity for others is likely to be counter-productive and invite the very situation it was intended to prevent.

Much of East Asia is at peace after many decades of conflict and tension. Most countries in the region, including China, are busy with economic development and modernization. China has a unique historic opportunity to become a modern prosperous great power, something which has eluded it for a century.

But it needs a peaceful and secure environment and the cooperation of the outside world to achieve this status. In the right conditions, China will be a mighty economic and military force in a few decades. Influence in Asia will then come naturally. It will be all the greater if China is also trusted and respected as a benign neighbour.

For the first time in more than a century, China is free of external domination or threat. In the past two decades it has come a considerable way in reintegrating itself with the outside world. But its reflexes and psychology are sometimes still those of a country beset by a hostile world.

China has to shed the baggage of history and come to terms with the realities of a modern, highly interdependent international community.

Much is now being done to help China understand this, but clearly it will take time for habits of thinking to change. The question is whether, before that happens, the region will spin into a vicious cycle of suspicion, tensions, declining economic cooperation and arms races.

The dangers in the South China Sea cannot be ignored. All parties to the disputes there should work towards a solution that accords with international rules and keeps the sea open to navigation and commerce.

Beijing's responsibility is clearly greater than that of the other parties. It is the only big power directly involved, it has far-reaching claims in the area, and it is a permanent member of the United Nations Security Council.

Note

This article first appeared in *International Herald Tribune*, 17 May 1995, under the title "Big China Needs to Behave Like a Good Neighbour".

22
On Balance, America is Benign

America has drawn much flak over the Iraq war. Many critics are men and women of honour. Yet some of the criticism makes the US appear a rogue state and a menace to world order. This is overdone. America's role in the world and in the Middle East today must be viewed in proper perspective and balance.

Ever since it became heavily engaged in global affairs from 1941, America has on the whole been a force for good. It played critical roles in saving the world from Nazism and communism. It set up a new international order after World War II based on multilateral institutions, security alliances and initiatives like the Marshall Plan to revive the economies of Western Europe.

America has made signal contributions to the security and economic well being of the Asia-Pacific region. Japan, South Korea, and Taiwan acquired their economic prowess under the American security umbrella and with access to the American market. It cost America over 30,000 lives to protect South Korea from a communist takeover in the early 1950s.

Together with Japan, America also fostered the economic development of Southeast Asia and helped the region to deal with the threat of communism. America's Vietnam venture in the 1960s and 1970s was controversial, but at that time it bought non-communist Southeast Asia precious time to develop its economic, political, and military strength so that it was better prepared to deal with the threat from communism in 1975 than it would have been in 1965.

To say that America is a benign power is not to say that it does not act in its own national interests. Of course it does. It is rather to say that it has often acted in enlightened self-interest that also benefits others.

Today, America remains the lynchpin of the Asian power balance and its overseas investments and access to its domestic market have been important drivers of Asian economic expansion. Only America had the power and resources to remove the Taleban regime in Afghanistan which had provided sanctuary for Al-Qaeda and where hundreds of militants from Southeast Asia had been trained. Imagine how much more difficult it would be for countries like Malaysia, Singapore, Indonesia and the Philippines to fight terrorism if training and support for terrorists had continued from Afghanistan.

Sept 11, 2001 scarred the American psyche and left it with an unprecedented sense of vulnerability to terrorists. This explains in large part President George W. Bush's doctrine of pre-emption and the reported desire to reorder the politics of the Middle East. There are legitimate concerns about both which have been widely expressed by critics.

Yet it must be borne in mind that the world today faces a new reality: subnational groups like suicidal terrorists which cannot be deterred by traditional means. If the international community does not address this problem and find a collective solution, powerful countries like the US which have been the victims of terrorist attacks are likely to resort to unilateral pre-emptive action.

America has traditionally preferred to resort to military action at least with a coalition, if not with the blessings of the United Nations. Despite the rhetoric from Washington, that practice has not changed fundamentally. Military action without international support is costly and less assured of success.

As for the Bush Administration's presumed agenda for the Middle East, it must be said that the region, from North Africa in the west to Afghanistan and Pakistan in the east, has been plagued by worrisome developments, such as the rise of Islamic fundamentalism and radicalism, the use of aircraft hijackings and suicide bombings for political and strategic objectives, and the rise of rogue or radical states trying to acquire weapons of mass destruction.

In a globalized age, these developments can no longer be dismissed as only of local consequence. America would be doing that region and the world a service if it can help to bring about change for the better, including a just settlement of the Israeli-Palestinian conflict. The question is whether such change can be brought about without prohibitive cost to the region and to America.

There are uncertainties and dangers ahead. The peace has yet to be won in Iraq and the divisions in the Western alliance arising from the war remain. It is too early to say if catastrophic terrorism has been curbed. However, failure is not pre-ordained and America's power to bring about beneficial change should not be underestimated.

The chances of a favourable outcome will improve significantly if America's initiative for the resolution of the Israeli-Palestinian conflict bears fruit. They will also be bolstered if, at this critical juncture, Europe works with the US instead of trying to create its own power centre as a counterweight to Washington. France and Germany must realize that, in the new reality of an enlarged Europe, the latter scheme is an empty dream.

In the end, the merits and demerits of the Bush Administration's policies on proliferation and rogue states will depend much on the outcomes — whether they make for a better Middle East and a better world. This is the ultimate moral and pragmatic measure.

Note

This article was first published in *The Straits Times*, 26 April 2003. Reprinted with permission of The Straits Times © Singapore Press Holdings Limited.

23
Resoluteness Alone Will Not Solve Bush's Security Woes

In Asia several governments have been pleased with the re-election of Bush as US President, in part because he is expected to be resolute on security issues.

But resoluteness, while necessary, may not by itself be sufficient to make progress in Iraq and the war on terrorism. There was ample resoluteness during the first Bush term, yet the international security situation has worsened in some important respects in the past two years. If the sorts of policy flaws witnessed over the past few years are repeated during the second term, the world could be a more dangerous place four years from now when Bush leaves office.

Iraq is turning out to be a major strategic setback, largely as a result of errors of judgment made by the Bush team about the post-invasion occupation and administration of the country. It has become an epicenter of terrorism, threatening the stability of the surrounding region, from where the world gets most of its oil, and America's power and prestige in the world.

Anti-Americanism has grown in the Muslim world, in part because of the perceived pro-Israel bias of the Administration which has complicated the fight against terrorism. America's alliances with key European states and its soft power have been damaged.

Even if the charge of unilateralism leveled by critics against this Administration is exaggerated, a deep impression has been created in significant parts of the world that the Administration is dismissive of the views of others on important international issues and determined to go its own way. In world affairs perceptions are an important reality with important consequences especially when they are about the sole superpower whose policies affect so many other countries.

The Administration's fiscal policies have been described by reputable economists as irresponsible. An impressive budget surplus inherited from the Clinton Administration has been turned into a huge deficit. If this trend continues, the resulting damage will not just be economic, both to America and the world, but also strategic. The world needs a strong America to fight the war against terrorism and to maintain the strategic balance; America cannot be strong if its finances are in shambles.

The disturbing feature about the first Bush Administration has been the primacy of ideology over pragmatic common sense in the conduct of policy in certain key areas. Some observers have argued that the lessons from past errors have been learned and that the second Bush term would be characterised by realism in the tradition of most other Republican presidencies after World War Two, including that of the elder Bush.

But there is no assurance yet that this will be the case. It is not clear if some of the influential figures of the current Administration have been willing to learn from past mistakes. There has been precious little accountability for failures in Iraq from an Administration that preaches to others the transformative powers of democracy. And the principal ideological support base of the Administration continues to be the pro-Israel Christian right and the neo-conservatives, making it difficult to reach out to the Muslim world.

During his second term Bush needs to move to a more centrist position to rally all Americans behind him and to put effort and energy into consulting and repairing America's image abroad. The fiasco in Iraq makes this all the more necessary. Condoleezza Rice's appointment as Secretary of State could hold promise because she would have the ear and the confidence of the President in a way that Powell probably did not. Hopefully the realist and internationalist part of her will not always succumb to ideology and she will be able to tell the President the way things really are rather than the way he wants to see them.

No country, however rich and powerful, can squander its wealth and energy by taking on too many burdens simultaneously, especially when this is done without enough international cooperation and support. The dictum attributed to Clausewitz that war is just diplomacy by other means should be taken to heart. Many a time it may be possible to achieve one's goals by means other than the direct use of military force on a large scale. In the war against terrorism, the political and psychological dimensions are crucially important. Resoluteness does not always need macho displays; more often it needs to be coupled with subtlety and sophistication based on a good understanding of situations.

The struggle against terrorism will be a protracted one, as will be the need to maintain a strategic balance in Asia. The sort of policies which have alienated allies, upset mainstream Muslims, led to the Iraqi quagmire and strained the US national treasury can only delight the terrorists and America's strategic rivals.

It is noteworthy that Osama bin Laden is reported to have said in a recent statement that his strategy is to bankrupt America. He said the mujahideen "bled Russia for 10 years, until it was forced to withdraw [from Afghanistan] in defeat... So we are continuing this policy in bleeding America to point of bankruptcy." Let us hope this remains just wishful thinking on the part of bin Laden.

Mercifully, the Administration's capacity to inflict more damage would seem to be limited by the consequences of policies pursued during the first term which have stretched the armed forces, especially the ground component, and busted the budget. But then who knows what will happen if ideology continues to prevail over realism.

Note

This article was first published in *The Straits Times*, 18 November 2004. Reprinted with permission of The Straits Times © Singapore Press Holdings Limited.

24
India Has a Key Role in Asia's Power Balance

In the game of Asian power politics, India has been receiving increased attention of late, being wooed in turn by America, China and Japan. India was geopolitically boxed in South Asia for four decades, in part as a consequence of the Cold War when its alignment with the Soviet Union caused the US and China, with the help of Pakistan, to contain it within the sub-continent, and in part because of its own economic and political mindset.

Economic and strategic challenges of the post-Cold War world have been changing India's old mindset and helping it to break out of its South Asian confinement. The opening up of the economy since the early 1990s has led to growth rates averaging around 6 per cent per year. A dynamic economy will provide the resources to pursue wider geostrategic interests. And the sea change in India-US security relations, especially since 9/11, has also made it easier for India to enter into closer political and security cooperation with America's friends and allies in the Asia-Pacific.

India still has many problems, but there is a new confidence that the country matters in the world and can achieve greater things. A richer India that is even partly freed from its preoccupation with South Asia, would be in a better position to pursue its oft stated security interests outside the land mass of the subcontinent. It has defined these, following in the footsteps of the British Raj, as stretching from Aden to Singapore, or as then Foreign Minister Jaswant Singh said in Singapore in June 2000, from the Persian Gulf to Southeast Asia including "an uninterrupted access to the Malacca Straits and the South China Sea".

India has a modest size navy with 38 principal combatants (destroyers, frigates, submarines and an aircraft carrier). According to present plans, their numbers will not increase significantly over the next decade, but their capability and reach will be expanding. For instance the navy is headed towards a force of two, and larger, aircraft carriers deploying MiG-29 aircraft. The first of these larger carriers, the refurbished *Admiral Gorshkov* of the Russian navy, is expected to enter service in 2008–2009 while a second carrier of similar tonnage will probably be deployed around 2015. There are indications that India also wants to develop a sea-based second strike nuclear capability.

The Indian navy has been cooperating with a number of Southeast Asian navies in training and exercises and has also carried out coordinated patrols with the Indonesian navy in the vicinity of the maritime border between the two countries. Many people may not know that the Indian navy has a Far Eastern Subcommand with its Headquarters in Port Blair in the Andaman Islands, which is near the northern entrance of the Straits of Malacca.

Of the three major suitors — America, China and Japan — whom will India favour? It is clearly to India's advantage to advance its relations with all three and it is doing precisely that. However, at the same time, it cannot be denied that the underlying quality of India's relations with each of these three powers remains different.

It is only natural for India to seek good relations with its giant neighbour China with which it shares a long land border. There are the business opportunities to exploit by expanding trade and commerce. There are also potent reasons for maintaining cordial political ties, not least because, from New Delhi's perspective, China retains the ability to be a spoiler in India's backyard, not just with Pakistan, but also in countries like Bangladesh and Nepal with whom India has problems. Despite the significant improvement in bilateral relations, suspicions of Beijing remain in the Indian political establishment while the attitude of the broader masses towards China is characterized by ignorance, laced with suspicion.

The attitude towards the US is clearly more favourable but still marked by some caution. The Indian political elite is well aware that the US has far more to offer to India, but is irked by what it regards as US indulgence towards Pakistan. The younger generation of Indians are much more fascinated by the West, especially America, notwithstanding their admiration for Japan's and China's achievements. The English language, the political and cultural pluralism, and the institutions inherited from the British draw India closer to the West. The influence of the Indian diaspora in the US, both in US domestic politics and in the high councils of India, should also not be ignored.

Japan seems to have just discovered India. The hitherto limited relationship can be expected to expand rapidly both economically and politically, partly because of belated

Japanese recognition of the changes that have been taking place in India, partly as a by-product of frictions in Japan's relations with China. There are also prospects of closer cooperation in the maritime sphere.

India's policies will ultimately be guided by what best serves India's interests. With its growing self-perception as a future great power, India would not want to be regarded as a mere handymaid of another great power.

Until a few years ago there was a widely held perception that China was likely to be the dominant power of Asia sometime later in this century. Today, because of the apparent determination of Japan to be a normal power (though in alliance with the US), the likely emergence of India, and the power that America still possesses to help shape the geopolitics of Asia in a direction it desires, the trends point more towards the eventual emergence of a multipolar power structure in Asia in which countries both cooperate and compete. But that may still be decades away; meanwhile America can be expected to remain the pre-eminent power.

Within such a multipolar configuration, whenever it emerges, there could well be a loose coalition of maritime powers like the US, Japan and Australia, together with India, seeking to balance China. Realists would of course find the emergence of a coalition of powers to balance any power that threatens to become too powerful as the most natural of occurrences. But in the Asian equation the shaping of such a coalition will require considerable political adroitness, hard work and patience. This is because China already has a clever strategy in place to prevent the rise of a meaningful balancing coalition through skilful regional diplomacy and by making key players economically dependent on it. Indeed how closely such a coalition jells will ultimately depend much on China's policies and actions in Asia.

Note

This article was first published in *The Business Times*, 10 June 2005.

25
China, Japan Must Meet and Talk More

The Sino-Japanese quarrel is not just about history. It is part of a deadly serious contest between the two countries for power and influence in the Asia of the 21st century.

From the mid-1970s, after China and Japan re-established diplomatic relations, till the late 1980s bilateral relations were reasonably amicable. But Sino-Japanese rivalry emerged in the 1990s, after the end of the Cold War. The disappearance of the Soviet Union removed a common enemy. The rise of China in the 1990s posed complex challenges for Japan which has been the leading Asian power for the previous half-century.

The advance of nationalism in both countries did not help either. China's new nationalism in the early 1990s, designed to shore up the legitimacy of communist party rule in an era when socialist ideology had lost its appeal, was based in part on glorifying the role of the party in defeating the much hated imperial Japanese army in China during World War II.

But China's constant hectoring of Japan about the latter's war time atrocities only stiffened Japanese attitudes. In such an atmosphere various incidents — whether concerning history, reported Chinese naval intrusions into

Japanese waters or territorial disputes — began to acquire greater salience. Acrimony and public opinion hardened on both sides.

Prime Minister Junichiro Koizumi has kept his election campaign commitment of five years ago to visit the Yasukuni shrine regularly. Among the more than two million Japanese war dead, the shrine also honours fourteen class A war criminals. So, in the process, Mr Koizumi has put himself into a straight jacket.

The visits could be damaging to Japan's international standing, especially at a time when it wants to become a more "normal" power with a stronger military. But Mr Koizumi is not stopping his visits in part because he is determined not to be seen to be bowing to China's pressure. Indeed some well wishers of Japan wonder why Japan is shooting itself in the foot in this way.

Over the past half century, through its aid and investments, Japan has contributed enormously to the economic development and modernisation of Asia, including Southeast Asia, much more than China. It still continues to do so. Yet it is not getting commensurate returns in terms of political influence. In recent years China's influence has grown significantly and is threatening to eclipse Japan's.

Some observers maintain that Japan's ineptitude partly accounts for this state of affairs. Tokyo, they argue, does not know how to meet the growing competition from China in Asia. While China comes out as a sophisticated operator which has thought through the next several moves, Japan appears as one lacking in strategic insight, giving the impression of flailing around, sometimes inflicting wounds on itself.

Nor is China coming up all roses from this brawl. There is the perception that it has been exploiting the Yasukuni and history issues to the hilt to advance its foreign policy and strategic objectives — for instance to deny Japan a permanent seat on the United Nations Security Council.

The actions of China, a potential super-power, are under close scrutiny in many countries. Its principles of a peaceful rise should be seen to apply to all countries, and not selectively.

China also needs to be mindful that half of Asia does not carry negative memories of Japan from the Pacific War. Japan's war against China lasted much longer than its war in Southeast Asia and was accompanied by much more destruction and suffering. Korea too suffered, having experienced four decades of unpleasant Japanese colonial rule.

But in Southeast Asia, the Vietnamese, the Thais, the Burmese, and the Indonesians do not have bitter memories of the Japanese. And India, which was not invaded and occupied by the Japanese, carries no anti-Japanese legacy from the war.

At this juncture both Japan and China need wise leadership. Tokyo needs to be more sophisticated in handling the sensitivities of neighbours and the competition from Beijing.

As for China, the question arises whether it is fully heeding Deng Xiaoping's advice that it should build up its power and wealth gradually, without making other powers feel insecure or threatened. It seems to be in a nervous hurry to advance its geopolitical interests, causing jitters among others in the process.

As some observers have noted, over the past decade, China has displayed a sort of wanton arrogance towards Japan, a great power in its own right, when a different, more respectful approach, might have been preferable.

ASEAN wishes to see all major powers play a positive role in building a peaceful and prosperous Asia, together with their ASEAN partners. A sense of respect for each other's role and contributions is essential if this enterprise is to succeed.

Perhaps the leaders of China and Japan should learn a piece of ASEAN wisdom — which is that they should continue to meet, discuss and play golf even when they have significant bilateral disputes between their countries. The northeast Asian leaders have obviously some way to go in emulating this salutary practice of their Southeast Asian friends.

Note

This article was first published in *The Straits Times*, 22 December 2005. Reprinted with permission of The Straits Times © Singapore Press Holdings Limited.

26
India's Ascent:
Rocky Path Ahead

India's rise as a great power could face more political and security challenges than is commonly appreciated. The South Asian region, with nuclear arsenals, is marked by deep seated inter-state enmities, political instability, religious extremism and terrorism. Indeed if terrorist groups were to acquire weapons of mass destruction India could be a prime target. Lately South Asia is also becoming an arena of sharper big power rivalry.

To be a great power on the Asian scene India needs to free itself from its South Asian quagmire. This requires, firstly, breakthroughs in its difficult relations with neighbours, especially Pakistan. Secondly, it also requires domestic peace and stability in South Asian countries. But, alas, both still appear out of reach. The momentum of the peace process with Pakistan seems to be petering out and growing instability in countries like Nepal, Sri Lanka, and Bangladesh has adverse implications for India's security.

The rising power of China is being increasingly felt in South Asia. Beijing accords much strategic significance to South Asia because of its energy lifelines through the Indian Ocean, and the perceived need to prevent India from joining any anti-China coalition sponsored by the United States.

Recently Beijing had New Delhi in a tizzy by seeking observer status in the South Asian Association for Regional Cooperation (SAARC). Some of India's neighbours — more interested in using SAARC to contain India than to cooperate with it — support this move.

Raja Mohan, a prominent Indian strategic affairs analyst, commented as follows on the recent SAARC summit in Dhaka where the issue of China's observer status came up: "As curtains came down today in Dhaka on the 13th SAARC summit, the event will be remembered only for the extraordinary demonstration of China's new political clout in the subcontinent. It was a long time coming. But when it did in Dhaka over the weekend China's diplomatic big bang left in tatters India's long standing claim of an exclusive sphere of influence in the sub-continent".

This could be China's riposte to India's growing strategic links with the US. It serves as a pointed reminder to India of its vulnerabilities in South Asia and how China could be spoiler, if need be, by exploiting them.

It would of course be preposterous to suggest that Beijing, like the terrorists, would seek to weaken India. After all, are the two countries not busy expanding their cooperation in various fields? But strategic temptation can be hard to resist when the stakes are high. So how India handles China and the reality of its growing influence in South Asia would be crucial. Since India cannot keep China, or for that matter the United States, out of South Asia it may be desirable to work with both these powers as well as the European Union to improve stability in India's neighbourhood.

On the Indian domestic front, in addition to cross-border terrorism in Kashmir and insurgencies in the northeast, there have been terrorist acts perpetrated recently in New Delhi and Bangalore. The sources of terrorism in India are the Pakistan based militant organizations, especially Lashkar-e-Toiba (LET) and the international jihadi movement. Still, there are disturbing signs that such acts of terrorism have recently been carried out with the assistance of some Indian Muslims. B. Raman, the well known Indian terrorism expert, has pointed out that "at least since 2003 their [the foreign terrorist organsiations] number is being augmented by a flow of volunteers from the Indian Muslim community, a phenomenon which should be of growing concern to our political leadership and security agencies".

India has almost 150 million Muslims, the second largest Muslim population in the world, larger than the population of either Pakistan or Bangladesh. Until recently it used to be said that none had been involved in jihadi terrorist organizations. If this is starting to change, does India have the capabilities to deal effectively with this threat which could focus on India's high tech sector?

New Delhi will have to face the new geopolitical and security challenges in an international environment in which the terrorist threat may be growing — from an expanding international Zarqawi network based in Iraq, a growing threat in Afghanistan where the terrorists seek to emulate tactics that have worked well in Iraq, and above all the threat of a global jihadi movement that Rohan Gunaratna has described as a "conglomerate of four dozen groups, linked ideologically, [that] will wage both local and global jihad campaigns world wide."

It is also an international setting in which the United States, because of perilous errors of judgment, has strategically weakened itself by overstretch in Iraq and the war against terrorism. Hence countries like Iran feel emboldened to defy the international community and jihadists worldwide may feel that the political wind is blowing their way.

To deal with the challenges New Delhi may have to move away from old stereotypes and adopt fresh, even bold approaches. The question is whether its leaders and its institutions, are ready and able to achieve such change. Better regional politics will pave the way for better economics which ultimately should be the principal driver of policies.

ASEAN-India cooperation has been expanding. New economic opportunities are unfolding, as well as prospects for closer security cooperation, especially in the maritime domain. ASEAN looks forward to a strong and confident India that is not bogged down in the seemingly intractable South Asian problems and is able to play a dynamic and positive role beyond its own region.

Note

This article was first published in *The Straits Times*, 21 January 2006. Reprinted with permission of The Straits Times © Singapore Press Holdings Limited.

27
America's Security Strategy and the "Long War" on Terror

It may sometimes be easier to fathom the foreign and security policy intentions of secretive states like China or even the Soviet Union of the Cold War than to figure out those of the United States. Power in Washington is dispersed between many agencies. Publicly released security policy documents are often written with different interest groups in mind, and may reflect compromises or scoring of points in turf battles, or attempts to impress Congress and public opinion.

Bearing this caveat in mind, certain observations may be in order on a few important policy documents on security that have emerged out of Washington this year, including the *2006 National Security Strategy of the United States* (NSS) and the *Quadrennial Defence Review*.

There is renewed emphasis on alliances and partnerships with other countries, reflecting a change from the previous unilateralist tenor. International circumstances, especially the experiences of Iraq and the war on terrorism, have propelled the change, as well as the severe budgetary constraints that the US Administration faces.

However this should not be misread as change in core values and thinking. The top people in the Administration in the run-up to the invasion of Iraq — President Bush,

Vice-President Dick Cheney, Defence Secretary Donald Rumsfeld, and Secretary of State Condoleezza Rice — are still there and the fifth who left, Colin Powell, was an ideological outsider. They are unlikely to have changed, within a few years, their deeply held core beliefs on global security and America's role in it. America's determination to remain the pre-eminent power and exercise global leadership also remains intact.

It seems clear that allies will be expected to share more of the security burdens in the future, though it is not clear to what extent they will be able to do so. NATO is already involved in Afghanistan and has assumed training responsibilities in Iraq. Australia is already described as a global partner in the long war. On India, with which US strategic cooperation is deepening, the NSS says it is "poised to shoulder global obligations in cooperation with the United States in a way befitting a major power."

The US sees the greatest threats to international security to be coming from *within* states because poorly governed states can become breeding grounds and sanctuaries for terrorists or arenas of domestic strife that can affect peace and stability of their surrounding regions. "Transformational diplomacy" will be used to bring about better governed, more democratic states in the critical areas of the world prone to conflict and terrorism.

There is much to be said for a long term strategy to deal with governance and state failure and to redirect America's diplomatic efforts to Asia and the Middle East. But the arenas of transformational diplomacy will be sovereign states. Though Rice says the US will work in the spirit of "partnership, not paternalism", she is unlikely to find easy partners to change domestic politics. And transformational diplomacy in Muslim countries will demand great subtlety for which this Administration has not exactly distinguished itself.

In a sense, the rhetoric of freedom and democracy that permeates the concept of transformational diplomacy, is not new. It has traditionally been an attractive part of American soft power, even if often with a touch of naivete. However, with this Administration the rhetoric seems to reach new heights, as if freedom and democracy were a panacea for all ills. This is a matter of some concern, given the recent history of poor judgments in relation to Iraq. One can only hope that no new folly is perpetrated under the misconception that democracy can be installed quickly in societies without the necessary institutions and traditions and that it will always bring about benign change.

Clearly the main national security preoccupation of the United States for many years will be the war on terrorism and preventing terrorists from acquiring weapons of mass destruction (WMD). It is still called a war, though critics have pointed out that such a portrayal of the struggle plays into the hands of the terrorists and encourages over-militarisation of the conflict on the American side.

The invasion of Iraq, the heavy-handed counter-insurgency tactics, and the continuing war hype by politicians and the media elevates the terrorists, generates anti-Americanism among the very Muslim communities in which the crucial struggle for hearts and minds has to be waged, and provides more recruits for the terrorists. Little wonder then, with mixed results after five years and no end in sight, the war has now been re-labelled as the "long war".

The policy documents do declare that the struggle against terrorism has to be waged by using a broad spectrum of national power — political, diplomatic, psychological and economic, apart from the traditional military and intelligence means — and that cooperation with other countries is crucial in this struggle.

But in practice there is still too much reliance on the military means. Iraq and Afghanistan provide almost daily examples of the use of aerial bombings which result in the loss of civilian lives and properties in collateral damage. The knowledge of other cultures and languages among operatives on the ground, necessary for an effective political and psychological effort, still remains weak, as Rice herself acknowledges.

Further, critics argue that budgetary priorities do not point to a balanced multi-dimensional effort against terrorism. They cite inadequate funding for such crucial areas as US port security, critical infrastructure protection in the US and preventing terrorists from gaining access to WMD, while the Defence Department receives six times the combined budget of the other agencies, even without including the costs of the wars in Iraq and Afghanistan.

Overall, the activism, the commitment and the resoluteness animating the various recent policy documents and statements are admirable. But there are also grounds for some concern. Wise states try to husband their resources, and, as far as possible, seek to achieve their objectives without fighting wars. The US is simultaneously fighting three wars — in Iraq, Afghanistan and the war against terrorism. It is committed to fight a fourth, of a different kind, in the Taiwan Straits, if the need arises. And, with an eye on China, it also seems determined to preserve its military pre-eminence in conventional warfare by developing expensive new weapons systems. All this is happening against the backdrop of a huge budget deficit and a falling dollar.

The US is also engaged in extensive worldwide efforts to prevent terrorists from laying hands on WMD. Yet according to a survey done in 2004–05 by Senator Luger of the Senate Foreign Relations Committee the estimated combined risk of a WMD attack (nuclear, chemical, biological or radiological) somewhere in the world within 5 years (ie by 2009) is 50 per cent and within the next ten years (ie by 2014) is 70 per cent.

Unless better progress can be demonstrated in the next few years and significantly more help obtained from allies, pressures could grow within the US for a different approach to fight the long war. Francis Fukuyama, who has in the past been connected with the neo-conservative movement, recently said "we need to demilitarize what we have been calling the global war on terrorism and shift to other kinds of policy instruments."

Note

This article was first published in *The Business Times*, 6 July 2006, under the title "Whither America's Long War on Terror?".

28
A Weaker America Could Allow the Quiet Rise of China

There is a decline in the clout of the United States in world affairs, especially in the Middle East. It is largely the result of the Iraq debacle, though other aspects of this US Administration's policies have also contributed to this.

Iraq has drained the strength of the all-volunteer US Army, leaving little ground forces capability for other contingencies. It is turning American public opinion against the war and may possibly be sowing the seeds of isolationism. The poor judgments and incompetence of US policy-makers have been on display before the whole world.

It is little wonder then that Iran can defy the international community about its nuclear programme and Hizbollah can confidently up the stakes in Lebanon. The fear of punishment from the only superpower seems to have dissipated. The confidence placed by key moderate Arab states in the US to secure the region's stability has been shaken. It is easy to understand their bitterness over US policies and their alarm over the rising power of Iran and the Shi'ites in the Persian Gulf.

Other countries too will be watching the unfolding drama closely. President Karzai in Afghanistan will be getting more nervous as the threat from the Taleban, with its sanctuaries in neighbouring Pakistan, grows. Pakistan's military regime may start to feel that it can continue to allow the Taleban to operate from these sanctuaries with impunity as well as tolerate an Al Qaeda presence so long as it does not threaten Islamabad's own vital interests. India will fear that externally-supported terrorism on its territory will grow. India-Pakistan rapprochement could come to a halt. Pakistan will likely be encouraged and India disheartened if a weakened US "hand" in South Asia results in a stronger Chinese one.

The last time the US was affected in this way was during and after the withdrawal from Vietnam in the 1970s, though the US posture on the critical Cold War military front in central Europe remained largely unscathed. When a war-weary US Congress cut off funds for any military operations in Vietnam and drastically reduced economic aid to then Saigon government, the North Vietnamese army delivered the coup de grace to the South Vietnamese regime.

Soon Cuban troops, together with Soviet combat advisers, were in Angola and Ethiopia. In December 1978 Vietnam invaded Cambodia and a year later the Soviets were in Afghanistan. After almost a decade of retreat, the US recovered its poise under the Reagan Administration. The concerns generated by blatant Soviet expansionism during a period of American weakness helped this recovery.

What of the Asia-Pacific this time around? Any weakening of the US posture in relation to the war on terrorism in critical zones like Iraq, Afghanistan and Pakistan, will embolden radicals and terrorists in Southeast Asia. On the broader Asia-Pacific canvas, the biggest beneficiary of any attenuation of US power and authority will probably be China. As the US, preoccupied with the Middle East, will have relatively little policy time for this part of the world, China will have even more latitude than it has been enjoying since 9/11 to advance its influence. The US, being in no position to confront North Korea over the nuclear issue, may have to acquiesce more in China's approach to the problem.

Will China take advantage of the situation to engage in expansionism in the way the Soviets did in the 1970s? That will probably not be its preference; some would say not even its style. Crude expansionism will alarm Asians and stir the giant on the other side of the Pacific into a vigorous response. In the maritime theatre that the Asia-Pacific is, the US will still have formidable military capabilites. China's strategy will likely be to encourage the weary giant of the Eastern Pacific to relax, even to allow its interests to be "taken care of" by China. In its goal to be the eventual Number One, China would ideally prefer a velvet transition, like a runner gracefully taking over the baton from one who has become exhausted after completing his run.

All this does not mean China is more "peace-loving" than other great powers. Indeed it has in the past shown itself quite capable of using force to advance its interests. It is perhaps only more sophisticated.

Pax Americana has served the world well for six decades, providing the stability and the international rule of law under which prosperity has spread and poverty has been reduced. It is of course premature to write it off, because, after all, the US will remain militarily, economically and technologically superior to any other power for many years to come.

But we seem to be entering a period in which America's capacity to persuade and have its way is likely to diminish. How long this phase will last is uncertain. Judging from the difficulties in extricating responsibly from Iraq, it is not even clear yet how far the position of the US will worsen before it gets better. Hopefully, it will recover some time in the future.

Note

This article was first published in *The Straits Times*, 18 December 2006. Reprinted with permission of The Straits Times © Singapore Press Holdings Limited.

29
ASEAN as a Geopolitical Player

ASEAN is viewed variously as an organization for regional confidence building, economic cooperation, or just a talk shop, depending upon the knowledge and disposition of the beholder. But not many people outside elite circles think of it as a geopolitical player. Yet, ASEAN has such a role. It has always wanted to influence the shape of the regional order and the role of major powers in it.

At one time there was a strong impulse among a few ASEAN members to keep the major powers out of Southeast Asia. This sentiment was reflected in the 1971 Zone of Peace, Freedom and Neutrality (ZOPFAN) Declaration, a document still cherished in the ASEAN pantheon, but now regarded more as a declaration of the region's desire to be the primary arbiter of its own fate. By the time the Cold War was over, it was clear to all ASEAN members that the major powers could not be kept out of Southeast Asia: rather ASEAN should seek a balance of their interests in the region.

The ASEAN Regional Forum (ARF) was set up in 1994 to address strategic and security concerns that arose after the end of the Cold War. These included the challenge of how to enmesh a rising China into the regional system and get it accustomed to international norms, and how to further anchor the US in the region and get it involved in a multilateral security framework. The ARF has remained a key vehicle for ASEAN's efforts to shape the geopolitical order in Southeast and East Asia. But it is not the only one. Others include the dialogue relationships with outside powers, the ASEAN Plus Three set-up, and the East Asian Summit.

Perhaps no single document spells out explicitly and comprehensively the contents of ASEAN's geopolitical vision for the region. However, broadly speaking, it is reasonable to say that ASEAN seeks:

a) Absence of hostility between the major powers, especially the US, China and Japan because it will adversely affect stability, and consequently, the economic prospects of the region. However, at the same time, ASEAN may not want a concert of major powers which would limit Southeast Asia's options — as the old adage goes, the grass gets trampled whether the elephants fight or make love.

b) A balance of the influence and interests of the major powers so that none is too dominant in the region

c) Benign and cooperative policies of the major powers towards the other smaller countries of the region.

The sceptic may ask: how can a group of ten relatively small countries aspire to manage the geopolitics of a region that is stalked by military or economic giants like America and Japan and rising behemoths like China and India with populations of one billion each?

ASEAN is not without some levers of influence, if it uses them skillfully. Perhaps the ASEAN region's most important asset is its strategic location astride the sea lanes between the Indian and Pacific Oceans which are critically important to the major powers for commerce and military passage. Second, with a growing market of over 550 million people, substantial natural resources, and a combined GDP of nearly a trillion US dollars, the ASEAN region is not insignificant economically. Third, ASEAN's position in the "driver's seat" of key organizations like the ARF, ASEAN Plus Three and the East Asian Summit gives it some clout to help shape the regional order in consultation with the big players. It is because of these factors that ASEAN is being courted by the major powers as they compete for influence in the region, a competition that ASEAN can also exploit to its advantage.

ASEAN believes that its vision of a regional order is in the interest of all major powers because it provides each one of them a legitimate stake in the region. As Prime Minister Lee Hsien Loong said in his ASEAN Day lecture on 7 August 2007: "Asean is non-threatening, enjoys good relations with all the major powers, and provides a neutral core around which to develop the regional architecture."

How successful ASEAN will be in realizing its geopolitical aspirations will depend partly upon how united ASEAN is. A divided ASEAN will obviously be less capable of dealing with the machinations of the major powers. But ultimately there will of course be matters beyond ASEAN's control. At the moment the constellation of stars, as it were, of big power relations seems aligned more in favour of ASEAN's aspirations, with all major actors seeing it to be in their interest, for their own different reasons, to avoid conflict. There is no guarantee that this will always be so. ASEAN's prescriptions are based on good sense, a measure of peer pressure and moral suasion, without any force to back them.

ASEAN-sponsored institutional structures are built on a sub-structure of power arrangements in which the US security presence has had a vital role for many years. The whole edifice could be destabilized in the future by possible crises in US-China or in China-Japan relations or a US military withdrawal from East Asia of a kind which upsets the regional balance and leads to a scramble for power and influence among the rising and resurgent powers. Such crises could also have their origin in domestic developments like the rise of nationalism or isolationism.

However, barring such bleak scenarios, globalization has greatly increased interdependence between the major powers and they are aware that conflict between them would be vastly destructive. If ASEAN can get its act together, it may be able to play an important role in helping to keep the peace. Without ASEAN and ASEAN-related structures, the rivalry between the major powers would be sharper and moré destabilizing to the region.

Note

This article was first published in *The Straits Times*, 22 August 2007. Reprinted with permission of The Straits Times © Singapore Press Holdings Limited.

30
China: A Powerhouse in Search of Grace

Visiting Shanghai and neighbouring Jiangsu province, it is difficult to avoid the feeling that a titan is rising. The energy of the people and the infrastructure bear witness to China's great strides forward. Communism did much damage, but it also accelerated the emancipation of women and provided free and compulsory education of nine years for both boys and girls. China's on-going historic transformation, a wonder to behold, has already lifted hundreds of millions out of poverty in just three decades.

Yet, while the modernization of hardware has leapt ahead, the software, as it were, perhaps unsurprisingly, lags behind. The highways of Shanghai are world-class, but motorists using them frequently flout traffic rules. Pedestrian crossings are provided for the security and safety of pedestrians but motorists believe they have the right of way, making crossing of roads, especially for the elderly, a serious hazard.

It is puzzling that some condominiums in Shanghai, a city considered relatively safe to live in, are ringed by conspicuous live electric wire fences mounted on concrete walls. Is it to enhance security or to flaunt their exclusiveness? Whatever the reason, they could have a divisive effect because they are said to annoy many ordinary people, and thus are not conducive to the government's stated goal of achieving a harmonious society. Another oddity is that in Jiangsu province the fees for entry to some of the historic and cultural sites seems way too high for the average Chinese. For instance it costs 90 yuan (S$17) to enter the Pingshan temple in Yangzhou, as much as a comfortable First Class train ride from Shanghai to Zengchiang, a distance of about 200 kilometers. The trishaw-man in Yangzhou gets 3 yuan for ferrying a passenger (or two) for 10–15 minutes.

Deng Xiao-ping's slogan to let some people get rich first may have been too successfully implemented, needing mid-course adjustment to deal with growing inequalities. The ugly aspects of capitalism in a system characterised as socialism with Chinese characteristics can be starkly visible.

Summer or winter, migrant workers from the countryside can be seen at night sleeping under flyovers in Shanghai. Although there is a minimum wage, said to be 850 yuan in relatively prosperous Shanghai, and lower in many of the provinces, it is not uncommon for employers to pay less for lower-skilled workers such as cleaners because of the abundant labour supply for that sector. And the rule that workers should get double the normal wage for working on public holidays seems as much honoured in the breach as the observance, the culprits being private employers contracted by local authorities to do cleaning or construction jobs.

Corruption, a huge challenge, often involves an unholy alliance among the local authorities, bankers and developers. There is some expectation that President Hu Jintao will deal with it more seriously, now that he appears to have consolidated his power.

What can be done? Liberals think a free press to expose wrongdoings is an essential requirement for a large country like China. Perhaps. But there is free press in the Philippines where many journalists are intimidated or murdered every year for reporting crooked affairs. Has it seriously reduced corruption? Even in China, when provincial newspapers report wrongdoings, the journalists are often harassed and threatened.

Sound institutions, effective rule of law and generally good governance have to go hand in hand with a responsible free press for this cancer to be seriously curbed. Education will have to play an important part in this. A friend once pointed out that in China's case something more is needed — the shaming of the corrupt — because at present there seems to be no shame involved in being corrupt, so common and acceptable a practice it has become. It is as if the legitimization of accumulation of wealth has also legitimized graft.

Traditional values and culture suffered severely during Mao Zedong's rule. China is setting up Confucian institutes in other countries to extend the reach of its soft power. Perhaps there needs to be a revival of ethics and morality within China to pave the way for a more harmonious society in this great country.

Note

This article was first published in *The Straits Times*, 9 November 2007. Reprinted with permission of The Straits Times © Singapore Press Holdings Limited.

31
Security Treaty Signals Closer Canberra-Jakarta Ties

In a joint declaration in 2005, Prime Minister John Howard and President SB Yudhoyono described the Australia-Indonesia relationship as "one of the most far reaching, high level interactions between two countries in the Asia-Pacific."

The new Australia-Indonesia security agreement which came into force on 7 February 2008 symbolizes this vastly improved relationship since its lows in 1999 over Australia's intervention in East Timor (Timor-Leste). Known as the Agreement on the Framework for Security Cooperation or the Lombok treaty — first signed by the two Foreign Ministers in Lombok, Indonesia in November 2006 — it is meant to maintain the momentum in relations and to further institutionalise the security dimension.

As a framework agreement, the Lombok treaty draws together different aspects of the extensive on-going security cooperation and provides the basis for the conclusion of other arrangements whenever deemed necessary by both parties. Apart from building defence relations, the treaty emphasises cooperation in non-traditional security, principally in relation to terrorism and transnational crime. Other areas covered include maritime security, a priority concern for Australia, and nuclear cooperation for peaceful purposes and for nuclear non-proliferation.

What has brought about this sea-change in Australia-Indonesia relations in recent years?

One crucial catalyst was the emergence of a common terrorist threat from Islamic radicals after 9/11 which forged a closer partnership between the police forces, immigration officials and security and intelligence services. Australia has assisted Indonesia significantly in counter-terrorism, including in post-bombing investigations and capacity building in a broad range of areas.

The other important catalyst has been the changing geopolitical landscape in Asia because of the rising powers, especially China, which have been actively seeking to expand their influence. Indonesia wants to maintain its strategic autonomy in the face of the new challenges and it suits the interests of Australia and the West to assist it to do so and to strengthen their own links with Jakarta. Although the Suharto era is gone, the present ruling circles in Jakarta are adhering to the long standing foreign policy of active independence and non-alignment, with a measure of quiet tilt towards the West. In the strategic geography of Asia, Australia remains a fulcrum of the Western strategic/military interests, even as it seeks to pursue its own economic and security interests.

The text of the Lombok treaty makes no mention of mutual defence that was implied in discreet language in the 1995 treaty negotiated between President Suharto and the Keating government which was unilaterally torn up by the Indonesians in 1999 when bilateral relations soured.

The 1995 treaty was apparently spurred by tensions in the South China Sea and the implications of China's claims in that sea for Indonesian territory. Since then the South China Sea issue has been anaesthetized, at least for the time being, and Jakarta's relations with China have improved and expanded, in tandem with those of other regional countries. Though underlying wariness and suspicions about China will likely persist in Jakarta, it has no desire or need, at least as of now, for a similar explicit mutual defence clause in the Lombok treaty.

Given Indonesia's domestic sensitivities over its past experience with Australia on Timor-Leste and the present simmering separatist sentiment in its Papua province, the Lombok treaty embodies a mutual undertaking not to support activities which constitute a threat to the stability or territorial integrity of either party, "including those who seek to use its territory for encouraging or committing such activities, including separatism, in the territory of the other." Yet Indonesia probably realizes that in practice such a commitment cannot be absolute and unconditional, especially since it is made subject to domestic laws and international obligations of both countries, with the implication that both have human rights obligations under international law.

In view of the continuing antipathy to Indonesia among the media and some other circles in Australia, it is interesting that the Australian Parliament's Joint Committee on Treaties has recommended that the government engage in a campaign to increase public support for the Australia-Indonesia relationship, including increasing awareness of democratic reforms in Indonesia and the value to Australian security of strong relations with Indonesia.

Australia's security role in the region has been multi-faceted and positive. Given Indonesia's geopolitical position in Southeast Asia and its role in ASEAN, Australia's contributions to its stability and progress also benefit ASEAN. Meanwhile, Australia remains part of the Five Power Defence Arrangements which include Malaysia and Singapore and has maintained traditionally close bilateral cooperation with both countries. It is playing a crucial stabilizing role in the South Pacific islands and in Timor-Leste where it has deployed troops. Its security assistance to the Philippines, like that to Indonesia, is specially important in the fight against terrorism in Southeast Asia.

These are impressive undertakings for a country of only 20 million people (though a GDP about 70 per cent of the combined ASEAN GDP), which has also deployed troops in Afghanistan and Iraq.

Note

This article was first published in *The Business Times*, 13 March 2008.

32
The Wagah Border:
From Division to Bridge

The residents of the city say there are only three places worth visiting in Amritsar: the Sikh Golden Temple, Jallianwalla Bagh where British Brigadier Dyer in 1919 massacred unarmed Indians — and the Wagah border. Indeed the flag-lowering ceremony at the end of each day on the India-Pakistan border at Wagah in Punjab has over the years become a tourist destination, attracting predominantly Indians and Pakistanis on the respective sides of the border, with a sprinkling of foreigners.

The Wagah check-point is about mid-way between the cities of Lahore in Pakistan and Amritsar in India, each about 25 kilometers away, on the only road link between the two neighbours. Here the border is marked in white as it cuts across the historic Grand Trunk Road (GTR). The road has been closed for years now at Wagah by two metal gates, one on each country's side. The two flag posts are located contiguous to the boundary line between the two gates.

Traditionally the flag-lowering ceremony has been a display of macho and mutual hatred by the border security forces on each side, though the animosity has been toned down in recent years. As the guards muster on each side and the crowds on both sides wave their respective flags, the air resonates with nationalistic slogans, including "Pakistan Jindabad ("Long Live Pakistan") and "Jai Hind ("Long Live India"). On the Pakistani side, there is also the intermittent playing of Koranic verses.

Then, at the appointed time, both gates are thrown open, the border troops take giant exaggerated steps towards the flag posts and stamp the ground vigorously with their boots. Their demeanor and facial expressions signify determination, defiance, even hostility. After the flag lowering, the two gates are shut with a loud clang, as if to signify a determination that each country will remain shut to the other.

A South Korean visitor on the Pakistan side of the border last year could barely contain his amusement over what, to him, looked like a farce. In his derisory merriment he forgot that it was perhaps no more farcical than the face-off between South Korean and North Korean troops at the Panmunjom on the 38th parallel border between the two countries.

Among the Indian and Pakistani crowds the ceremony seems to arouse tangled emotions, a mix of sadness, hostility, curiosity and perhaps a yearning to connect. I observed the hostility and tragic pathos last year on the Pakistani side: an old bearded man was trotting up and down the 30 metres of GTR enclosed by the public stands, shouting slogans and waving a Pakistani flag. I was told he was eighty, lived nearby, had lost two sons in wars with India, and performs this demonstration everyday during the flag lowering ceremony.

But there are those who have seen enough of politics and wars and are immensely saddened by the futility of sustaining such hatred. After all, the flat landscape, the rolling brown wheat fields of April, broken by occasional clumps of trees, were identical on both sides of the border; the people, though of different faiths are the same too; and the birds flew freely from one side to the other oblivious of the man-made barriers and the grotesque displays of physical and psychological divisions.

At the end of the ceremony each day, the crowds on both sides flock near the boundary fence and peer intently and curiously at the other side. What unspoken emotions, what forces in the conscious and the subconscious propel them to do so?

The Indian province of Punjab, which Senior Minister Goh Chok Tong visited recently, is India's richest province, but it is only a small fraction of the pre-partition Punjab. It was then a land of five rivers and stretched from Delhi to Peshawar on the northwest frontier of today's Pakistan. The present Indian Punjab, with a population of about 25 million, emerged from two partitions: between Pakistan and India in 1947, and, in 1966, of the Indian Punjab into the three provinces of Punjab, Haryana and Himachal Pradesh as a result of Sikh demands for a Punjabi-speaking province.

In view of the thaw in relations between India and Pakistan in recent years, there are hopes that border might be opened up and there can be people-to-people and business-to-business links with Pakistani Punjab. The revival of the forces of democratization in Pakistan further encourages such hopes. When that does materialize, the absurdities of Wagah will be relegated to the dustbin of history. Common sense, together with the sense of a common Punjabi identity, could contribute to the breaking of barriers between India and Pakistan at this epicenter of the divide between the two countries.

Note

This article was first published in *The Straits Times*, 26 April 2008. Reprinted with permission of The Straits Times © Singapore Press Holdings Limited.

33
Fix the Gaping Holes in India's Security

The scale and nature of the Mumbai terrorist attacks bring into sharp relief the failures of the Indian intelligence services. They either did not have prior information of the attacks or they did not follow up on leads. The central intelligence services are short of resources while the local police forces are less than effective in counter-terrorism work. Analysts have also noted weaknesses in maritime security and the lack of coordination among the different security agencies.

It is surprising that this state of affairs exists, considering that India has long been an obvious target of extremist groups based in Pakistan. Indian officials often lament that they have been the victims of terrorism longer than almost any other country in the world. That is true. So why haven't they been willing or able to get on top of the problem?

If the Mumbai attacks lead to the country's counter-terrorism structures being reformed and revitalised, they would be a blessing in disguise. But do not bet on it. If the past is any guide, investigative commissions will be set up but their recommendations will be ignored or only weakly followed up. It is much easier to blame Pakistan or groups in Pakistan and leave it at that, as if that absolves the Indian government from putting its own house in order.

This is not to say that Pakistani groups were not involved in the Mumbai attacks. In all probability, they were, possibly with the help of Muslim Indians. But this should not be used as an excuse not to do what needs to be done to better secure India from terrorist attacks.

Indians are justly proud of the resilience of their society. But there is danger that if terrorists can repeatedly attack vital or iconic facilities with impunity, they may be able to inflict serious damage on India's prospects, notwithstanding the resilience of ordinary Indians.

Over the long term, the greatest danger India faces comes from home-grown terrorist groups, with or without the assistance of Pakistani-based groups. It is still not known if any of the Mumbai attackers were Indian nationals or how much local support they had. India's rise as a great power could be seriously constrained if India-based Islamist groups gain momentum, adding to the already formidable list of internal security problems the country faces.

Beyond the shortcomings of the country's intelligence and security services, there are also deficiencies in governance and the rule of law. In a multi-religious society like India, religious issues need to be addressed with great care and sensitivity. Incidents like the demolition of the Babri mosque in Ayodhya in 1992 and the anti-Muslim Gujerat riots of 2002, in both of which the opposition Bharatiya Janata Party was implicated, helped to provide recruits for indigenous extremist groups. The failure of the government to bring to justice the perpetrators of these crimes, no other word would do, would no doubt have fired many Muslim youths with a deep sense of injustice.

The country's major political parties have continued to play the religious card to win popularity and votes. Critics have argued that the present Congress government has been reluctant to appear to be tough on terrorism for fear of alienating the Muslim community whose votes it has been courting. The fight against terrorism must be insulated from such political considerations and prosecuted vigorously with adequate laws that apply to all communities without fear or favour.

Indians sometimes argue that their democracy has always been messy but that has never prevented them from somehow muddling though various challenges. They point to the strong sense of unity in the country, confident that the vast majority of Muslim Indians will not be attracted to extremism.

Perhaps. But it will be unwise to take things for granted. The world around India has changed much since Sept 11. There is now an international radical Islamist movement, its message easily accessible over the Internet. Next-door Pakistan harbours Al Qaeda as well as a number of Pakistani extremist groups associated with Al Qaeda. India's strategic cooperation with the US and its economic successes add grist to the mill.

Note

This article was first published in *The Straits Times*, 2 December 2008. Reprinted with permission of The Straits Times © Singapore Press Holdings Limited.

34
Chiang Kai-shek's Legacy Lives On in China

A side trip from Shanghai recently took me to Xikou near the port city of Ningbo in Zhejiang province. An otherwise non-descript place in the countryside, its claim to fame rests on it being the birth-place of Chiang Kai-shek, who ruled China in the 1930s and 1940s. Tour coaches disgorge loads of visitors, mostly Chinese and Taiwanese but also some other foreigners, who travel here to view the Chiang family residences.

The residences have largely survived the upheavals of the Chinese civil war and the Cultural Revolution. Parts that were damaged have been restored. In 1949 Mao had instructed that his arch-enemy's properties in his home village not be violated, suggesting he saw political value in such restraint.

Indeed, the Kuomintang and the Chinese Communist Party, despite their hostility, maintained on-off secret contacts during Mao's rule, and reportedly held inconclusive secret peace talks in the early 1960s. When China plunged into the chaotic Cultural Revolution in the mid-1960s, the People's Liberation Army made Xikou a protected area, though official communist propaganda continued to vilify Chiang as a traitor.

The main residence and three other buildings which the Chiang family used are scattered in the vicinity of a small river and command a good view of the picturesque hills near by. There are no slogans, no propaganda, no attempt to besmirch Chiang. The buildings include the quarters of Chiang's eldest son, Ching-kuo. His mother, Chiang's first wife, was killed in a Japanese air raid on Xikou in 1939. A small stone tablet erected by Chiang Ching-kuo bears an inscription vowing revenge.

By and large, the complex is spared the crass commercialization of tourist sites by the local authorities that one often encounters in China, except for one unfortunate lapse: Next to one of the buildings is an enclosure for dog fights: for 100 yuan (S$22) you can watch a fight for 8 minutes, a spectacle at odd surely with the reflective ambience of the historic site.

There are indications that many ordinary Chinese now view Chiang as a nationalist and an important figure in modern Chinese history. We asked our young driver, a Ningbo resident, what he thought of the generalissimo. "He was a good man", he responded without hesitation, adding, after a slight pause "also a great man." When asked why Chiang was great, he pointed to the Chiang residences and said, with a smile: "Go and see for yourself."

It is not too hard to see what would have appealed to our driver and other Chinese visitors to the residences. On pictorial display was Chiang's role in unifying a China divided by warlords, his nationalism and even his struggle against the Japanese.

Also, the modesty of the buildings stood out. The furniture, photographs and captions convey the image of a simple, unostentatious man steeped in Chinese traditions and culture. Included in the display, in Chiang's own handwriting (in classical Chinese) are moving tributes to his grandfather, father and mother on the occasions of their deaths. To many Chinese the residences would stand in refreshing contrast to the extravagant lifestyles and lack of traditional virtues among today's rich.

This partial and quiet rehabilitation of Chiang is still too touchy a subject for Beijing to acknowledge openly. But though limited, it is a welcome step in the direction of a more mature and fair accounting of history.

Will it remain confined to Chiang's role, given its significance in the mainland's relations with Taiwan? Or does it also augur an opening up in other sensitive aspects of the country's history — the 1989 Tiananmen student uprising, say, or the role of then CCP general secretary Zhao Ziyang?

China's current leadership probably realizes that to be a self confident great nation, the country eventually has to come to terms with its past. The critical determining factor in deciding the degree of openness will be the leadership's assessment of how openness can be achieved without undermining national stability and the continuity of communist rule.

Note

This article was first published in *The Straits Times*, 4 May 2009, under the title "Chiang Kai-Shek's Legacy Lives On". Reprinted with permission of The Straits Times © Singapore Press Holdings Limited.

35
Asia-Pacific Security: The Danger of Being Complacent

The Asia-Pacific region has enjoyed generally stable and peaceful relations between the major powers for over two decades. Sino-Japanese relations have improved, there is better US-China cooperation on a range of issues, and economic interdependence among the major powers has increased greatly. There is unprecedented dialogue, both bilaterally and in ASEAN-anchored multi-lateral organizations.

Yet the regional situation is not without its troubling features. There is significant military build-up; and political and economic competition, not always of the healthy kind, could intensify in the coming years. Some observers also note a more assertive Chinese posture from the South China Sea to the Sino-Indian border and wonder if Beijing is trying to take advantage of America's economic straits and its dependence on Chinese cooperation to advance China's interests. Meanwhile, the two old potential flash points — the Korean peninsula and Taiwan — remain flashpoints, though the latter seems to be on the back-burner for now.

China's on-going build-up of military capabilities — which include a major base on Hainan island that could house strategic nuclear as well as conventional attack submarines and is uncomfortably close to the vital sea lanes of Southeast Asia — has already drawn a response from Australia. It has come up with its own defence modernization plan for the next couple of decades and plans to build a dozen long range attack submarines and buy 100 Joint Strike Fighters from the US.

The recently issued Australian Defence White Paper indicates Canberra's concerns: "It would be in our strategic interests in the decades ahead that no power in the Asia-Pacific region would be able to coerce or intimidate others in the region through employment of force, or through the implied threat of force, without being deterred, checked or, if necessary, defeated by political, economic or military responses of others in the region."

For its part, the US has been strengthening its alliances with Japan and Australia, stepping up its military presence in Guam, and increasing strategic cooperation with India — moves that Beijing tends to see as attempts to fence it in.

Likewise, there are concerns in New Delhi that China is stepping up its apparent encirclement of India by supporting Pakistan militarily, strengthening ties with other South Asian states, and putting pressure along the disputed Sino-Indian border. So there is insecurity — and even streaks of paranoia — all round.

It is true the major powers of today do not seek conflict with one another. The destructive potential of war makes it counter-productive. Besides, the major powers have more important national priorities to attend to.

However, while conflict is unlikely, it is not unthinkable or impossible, especially in an Asia-Pacific environment where deep insecurities lie just beneath the surface. The temptation to exploit a strategic opportunity, domestic compulsions or the fear of loss of face are among the factors that can cloud rational judgment and lead to miscalculation. Even a limited conflict triggered off in this way could seriously damage the web of vital relationships in the region.

Economic interdependence does not by itself avert conflict when perceived vital national interests or prestige is at stake. The great wave of globalization preceding World War I did not prevent the outbreak of hostilities, though it was widely believed that it would.

In his book *The Ascent of Money,* Harvard historian Niall Ferguson wonders: Why were many thinking people of the time so oblivious to the possibility of World War I when, on hindsight, there were so many factors propelling the great powers towards conflict?

His take: "The combination of global integration and financial innovation had made the world seem reassuringly safe for investors. Moreover it had been thirty four years since the last major European war, between France and Germany, and that had been mercifully short."

He draws two important lessons: First, that major wars can arise even when economic globalization is highly advanced; and second, "the longer the world goes without a major conflict, the harder one becomes to imagine (and, perhaps the easier one becomes to start)."

This is not to uncritically endorse Professor Ferguson's views nor to suggest that Asia is fated to repeat Europe's history. It is only to argue against complacency and point to the dangers that exist despite the hard work by many to promote peace and security in the region.

Note

This article was first published in *The Straits Times*, 31 July 2009. Reprinted with permission of The Straits Times © Singapore Press Holdings Limited.

PART IV
Remembrances of Conflicts Past

36
Turning Point in the
Vietnam War

Forty years ago, on 31 January and 1 February 1968, Vietcong and North Vietnamese forces launched the Tet (Lunar New Year) offensive in cities and towns across South Vietnam. It was the first, and most dramatic, part of a three phase campaign. Fierce fighting raged in most of the provincial capitals as well as the national capital Saigon during early February.

The onslaught was intended to break the stalemate in the Vietnam war and stymie the mounting pressure from American forces by bringing about a "general uprising" in the South that would topple the Saigon government or at least result in negotiations to end the war on terms favourable to Hanoi.

But the offensive was repelled with heavy losses for the communists. They could not take any important town, except parts of Hue from which they were later ousted. The Vietcong in particular suffered such grievous losses that the war in the South was henceforth waged mainly by the North Vietnamese. The communist leaders had underestimated the mobility of American forces and misread the mood of the people. The general uprising they expected failed to materialize.

Yet the Tet offensive brought the communists success thousands of miles away from the battlefield, in Washington. Evidence from communist documents and post-war interviews with North Vietnamese commanders suggest that Tet's big impact on US domestic opinion was unexpected. Of course, when it did occur, Hanoi capitalized on it.

The offensive came as a shock to the American public because it had been led to believe that the war was being won and the communist side was progressively weakening. The American commanders had not understood the nature of the enemy they were pitted against and had underestimated his capabilities.

The anti-war movement already had significant traction among young Americans before Tet occurred. Now it received a big boost. Diverse interest groups joined forces with college students and pacifists to oppose the war. Most of the media too turned against it. Indeed this was the first "television war" in which stark images of battlefield scenes invaded American homes via TV cameras.

The change in US policy came with the realisation among policy-makers that the war could not be won, at least not within the self-imposed confines of a "limited war". (For instance policy-makers had ruled out an invasion of North Vietnam.) Any continuation of attempts to win would have entailed further sacrifices that the American people would not have been prepared to accept. It was clear by then that Hanoi's perspective on the level of pain and losses that it could absorb were quite different from Washington's.

On 31 March 1968 US President Lyndon Johnson announced a suspension of American bombing above 20 degrees north latitude — which meant most of North Vietnam

— and offered to open negotiations. He also announced that he would not seek re-election as president. It would take his successor four more years to gradually wind down American involvement in the war.

The Vietnam war was part civil war, part ideological conflict, and part a proxy war between the main protagonists in the Cold War. It also had a dimension of Sino-Soviet rivalry which came out more openly in Southeast Asia after its end. It was a hugely destructive war. More than a million North Vietnamese and Vietcong military personnel were killed or missing in action from 1960 to 1975; over 600,000 were wounded. Hundreds of thousands of South Vietnamese troops died. Estimates of civilian deaths in both Vietnams have ranged from half a million to a few million. There was a huge destruction of physical infrastructure from which Vietnam has yet to fully recover. After its victory in 1975, Hanoi was soon embroiled in conflict in Cambodia. The net result of its various wars was that Vietnam had thirty years of catching up to do with the ASEAN-5 in terms of economic development.

On the American side, nearly 60,000 troops died and over 300,000 were wounded. Policy-makers realized that, in the age of television and instant communications, an open democracy like America could not fight a protracted war in a distant land if there was no clear and immediate threat to American security, and certainly not with a conscript army.

Perhaps historians are still too close to the fateful events of the 1960s and 1970s to judge the merits of critical decisions taken then by both sides. History has its ironies and twists. Vietnam's former ally, China, which America thought it was trying to contain when it first entered the war, is today Hanoi's foremost external security concern while America is seen by Vietnam as a necessary balancer in Asia. And despite the horrors of the Vietnam war, there seems to be considerable goodwill among the Vietnamese, especially the young, towards America.

Note

This article was first published in *The Straits Times*, 4 February 2008. Reprinted with permission of The Straits Times © Singapore Press Holdings Limited.

37
The Malayan Emergency: Of Plots, Plotters and Protagonists

Sixty years ago this month, in June 1948, three British plantation managers near Sungei Siput in Perak were killed by insurgents of the Communist Party of Malaya (CPM). The killings marked the beginning of a violent communist insurrection in Malaya, which prompted Malaya's British colonial rulers to declare a state of Emergency in the country.

The insurgency lasted twelve years. It was a war of ambushes, assassinations, and fire-fights, with CPM insurgents attacking Malaya's transport and economic infrastructure. The insurgency greatly affected the lives of people, causing much hardship.

To the communists, "Malaya" included the peninsula and Singapore. The focus of the insurgency, however, was the peninsula. In Singapore, it focused on a united front strategy to seize control, from within, of organisations such as trade unions, student and cultural bodies and political parties — and occasionally resorting to assassinations.

Thousands of insurgents and security forces personnel, as well as over 3,000 civilians, died in the conflict. The cost of the Emergency to the Malayan and British governments ran into billions of Malayan dollars.

The British colonial government did not want to describe the conflict as a "war", possibly to safeguard morale in Malaya and Britain. So it continued to be called the Emergency. The insurgents were first called "bandits", then "communist terrorists" (CTs). But they saw themselves as freedom fighters, and called their army the Malayan National Liberation Army (MNLA).

The insurgency was broken with an integrated strategy that embraced police, military, civil operations and intelligence. A Special Branch (SB) of the police force was developed as the key intelligence agency. The bulk of its intelligence came from human sources — some of the best from captured and surrendered insurgents who had to be skilfully interrogated. Military intelligence did not have its own intelligence collection and worked instead under the SB.

Compare this with United States counter-insurgency operations in Iraq and Afghanistan today, with their over-reliance on military force, technical intelligence (leading sometimes to ghastly bombing errors) and interrogations of detainees subcontracted to mercenary private operators.

During the Emergency, the British made a concerted effort to separate the insurgents from their support base by resettling an estimated half a million Chinese squatters in the countryside in protected New Villages. Guerillas were supposed to operate like fish in water, according to Mao Zedong. The British strategy was to drain the water and leave the fish floundering.

As the military tide turned decisively against the CPM from 1954, the British authorities prepared Malaya for independence, thereby undermining the MNLA status as an anti-colonial liberation army. Tunku Abdul Rahman, the Chief Minister of Malaya, was able to negotiate confidently with CPM leader Chin Peng in Bali in December 1955 as the head of a multi-racial Malayan coalition that had won an overwhelming victory in the federal elections of July 1955. The Tunku was accompanied by the elected Chief Minister of Singapore, David Marshall. Sensing the adverse tide on the battlefield, the CPM wanted to return to its pre-1948 status as a legal party, free to participate in the political process. But the Tunku and the British refused to accept any settlement that would have allowed the CPM to continue its struggle for a communist Malaya through other means.

By 1960, the peninsula had been cleared of the insurgents and the Emergency ended. The CPM attempted to launch a come-back in the 1970s from its southern Thai sanctuaries. It was unsuccessful because Malaysia had changed by then — and so had the CPM's patron, China. By the late 1970s, after Deng Xiaoping assumed power in China, Beijing began withdrawing its support of communist movements in Southeast Asia.

The Malayan Emergency must be seen in the context not just of decolonization but also of the Cold War. Southeast Asia featured prominently in the calculations of Western powers during the Cold War.

Communism was seen be on the march in Asia in the 1940s and the 1950s, given Mao's victory in China in 1949, Vietminh advances in Vietnam, and North Korea's invasion of South Korea. There was genuine concern in Western circles that the Vietnamese communists would take over Indochina and resistance to communism in then-Burma and Thailand would collapse thereafter. Such concerns persisted through the 1950s. They intensified after the fall of Dien Bien Phu in 1954 which led to the establishment of the US-led Southeast Asia Treaty Organization (SEATO). Contingency plans were drawn up for the defence of Thailand in the event of a Chinese invasion. The growing strength of the Indonesian communist party to the south only added to the security anxieties.

Hence communism had to be defeated in Malaya. And it was — with patience, determination and skill. The CPM's limited support — it was confined largely to sections of the Chinese community — and the fact Malaya did not share a border with a revolutionary communist state, were also factors in the CPM's defeat.

British exertions in Southeast Asia in the sunset days of its empire — in helping to defeat the CPM insurgency as well as its defence of Malaysia against Indonesian Konfrontasi — served British interests in Southeast Asia. On the whole they also served well the interests of non-Communist Southeast Asia.

Chin Peng has lamented that the history written by his foes has not judged him fairly. Perhaps, but if he had been the victor, one wonders what would have happened to the foes.

Note

This article was first published in *The Straits Times*, 21 June 2008. Reprinted with permission of The Straits Times © Singapore Press Holdings Limited.

Acknowledgements

The articles reproduced in this book first appeared in:

ISEAS Trends:
- "Sino-Vietnamese Reconciliation: Cause for Celebration?" under the title "Sino-Vietnamese Embrace: Cause for Celebration?", July 1991.
- "Asia-Pacific Security Comes under ASEAN's Scrutiny", June 1993.
- "Where is Myanmar Headed?", April 1994.
- "What Indonesian Stability Means to the ASEAN Region", June 1997.
- "Democratic Peace Theory and Asia: The Jury is Still Out", June 1998.

International Herald Tribune:
- "East Asian Security Means Dialogue and US Will", 27 July 1993.
- "China Needs to Act Like a Good Neighbour", under the title "Big China Needs to Behave Like a Good Neighbour", 17 May 1995.
- "ASEAN's Achievements are Endangered by Continuing Crisis", 24 July 1998.

Business Times:
- "India Has a Key Role in Asia's Power Balance", 10 June 2005.

- "America's Security Strategy and the 'Long War' on Terror", under the title "Whither America's Long War on Terror?", 6 July 2006.
- "Pakistan Faces a Gathering Storm", *Business Times*, 3 August 2007.
- "Security Treaty Signals Closer Canberra-Jakarta Ties", 13 March 2008.

Straits Times:
- "The Changing Face of International Relations as America Combats Terrorism", under the title "Face of Future Global Ties as US Combats Terrorism", 22 November 2001.
- "Surprising, Squabbling, Peaceful ASEAN", 16 September 2002.
- "A Not so Happy New Year?", 2 December 2002.
- "There is Method to Howard's Madness", 6 December 2002.
- "Singapore's Stand on Iraq: Clear and Forthright", 18 March 2003.
- "On Balance, America is Benign", 26 April 2003.
- "Fast SARS Action Shows ASEAN Not Just a Talk Shop", 7 May 2003.
- "Sept 11: Two Years on, Southeast Asia Breaks Terrorism's Deadly Lock", 11 September 2003.
- "US Bungling Makes Iraq a Problem for the World", under the title "Why Iraq is Not Just America's Problem", 11 December 2003.
- "Iraq is Not Like Vietnam — For Now", 13 April 2004.
- "Losers and Winners in the Iraq War", 14 May 2004.

- "Resoluteness Alone Will Not Solve Bush's Security Woes", 18 November 2004.
- "Is Bangladesh Waking Up to Danger of Islamic Militancy?, under the title "Dhaka Wakes Up to Danger of Islamic Militancy", 7 April 2005.
- "China, Japan Must Meet and Talk More", 22 December 2005.
- "India's Ascent: Rocky Path Ahead", 21 January 2006.
- "A Weaker America Could Allow the Quiet Rise of China", 18 December 2006.
- "ASEAN as a Geopolitical Player", 22 August 2007.
- "China: A Powerhouse in Search of Grace", 9 November 2007.
- "Turning Point in the Vietnam War", 4 February 2008.
- "The Wagah Border: From Division to Bridge", 26 April 2008.
- "The Malayan Emergency: Of Plots, Plotters and Protagonists", 21 June 2008.
- "Southeast Asia Succeeds in Keeping Terrorism at Bay", under the title "ASEAN Succeeds in Keeping Terrorism at Bay", 4 August 2008.
- "Fix the Gaping Holes in India's Security", 2 December 2008.
- "Chiang Kai-shek's Legacy Lives On in China", under the title "Chiang Kai-Shek's Legacy Lives On", 4 May 2009.
- "Asia-Pacific Security: The Danger of Being Complacent", 31 July 2009.

Index

ABOUT THE AUTHOR

Daljit Singh is a Visiting Senior Research Fellow at the Institute of Southeast Asian Studies (ISEAS), Singapore. He has published extensively on regional security issues. His most recent book, an edited collection, is *Terrorism in South and Southeast Asia in the Coming Decade*. He is also the editor of *Southeast Asian Affairs*, the annual ISEAS review of Southeast Asia.